Advance Notice

Cutting Remarks is the account of one Vermont boy's intoxication with the raw power of the logging equipment he encounters in his first job in the woods: the whine of the chainsaw, the cloud of blinding, blue 2-cycle smoke, the storm of wood chips flying from the cutter bar, and finally his awe at seeing an eighty-foot pine tree crashing to earth.

Torrey is an accomplished storyteller and his oral skills translate beautifully into the written word. We are led through the life-threatening world of mountain side logging where a skidder or dozer can pitch over and crush its driver, a razor-sharp saw can remove a human limb faster than a tree limb, or the logger can misjudge the tree's fall and die under his own fell. Torrey takes us through the chaotic and deadly world of logging from planning an escape route, to finessing undercuts and back-cuts, and limbing and bunching a load of logs to be skidded to the landing.

But beyond the visceral and ever-present danger in this memoir lies the spiritual evolution of its narrator from brash, risk-seeking young woodsman into an older and more contemplative observer of the forest in which he makes his living. The adrenaline rush brought on by dropping 50-60 trees a day gives way to a stillness and respect for the life of a tree, the life in a tree, and the community of trees that make up a forest.

As the narrative progresses, Torrey evolves a sophisticated personal ethos of forest stewardship, management, and the significance of trees in our lives and in our environment. *Cutting Remarks* transcends its own drama to become a quiet story as much about trees and a way of living with and working among them as about logging, machinery, and danger… and therein lies its harmonious beauty.

I loved this book.   – Bill Schubart, author of *Lila & Theron*

Bill Torrey

Cutting Remarks

Forty Years in the Forest

191 Bank Street
Burlington, Vermont 05401

Copyright © 2019 by Bill Torrey

All rights reserved. No part of this publication may be reproduced, distributed, or transmitted in any form or by any means, including photocopying, recording, or other electronic or mechanical methods, without the prior written permission of the publisher, except in the case of brief quotations embodied in critical reviews and certain other noncommercial uses permitted by copyright law.

OnionRiverPress
191 Bank Street
Burlington, VT 05401

Printed in the United States of America

ISBN: 978-1-949066-28-9
Library of Congress Control Number: 2019911309

For more information visit the author's website:
www.billtorrey.com

Cover Painting by Kathleen Kolb
Book Design by WillmottStudios.com

To Keith Blake (Art),
but for whose love, courage and quickness
I would not be here.

Contents

It Ain't Rocket Surgery	11
Getting the Maine Idea	21
Back Home in the Land of Eden	25
The Art of Work	35
Sustainable Logging	43
The Chainsaw	49
Bulldozer Bunching	55
The Woods	63
Bound Up and Pinched Tight	67
Dead Trees Standing	75
Hell on Wheels	79
Back at It	83
Trouble Comes in Threes	87
The Lone Logger	95
A Hairy Story	99
Holy Moses!	105
Bolton Notch Ass-Backwards	111
Going to Town	119

I'll Be Dogged	123
Up Mount Philo the Hard Way	127
Shooting the Breeze	133
Paying the Dues	141
"A Man's Got to Know His Limitations"	147
Answering the Bell	153
The Waterworks	159
Mad River Glen- Log It If You Can	165
Shear Genius	175
Need a Tums?	181
Size Does Matter	187
A Rabble Alliance: May the Forest Be With You	191
Forward Into the Woods	203
Rolling Along	213
Kneeded In the Worst Way	221
At the End of The Haul	229

"The record shows
I took the blows
And did it my way"

– Paul Anka & Jacques Revaux

Chapter 1
It Ain't Rocket Surgery

It was early September and I had just turned twelve. I'd gotten a .410 shotgun for my birthday in August and I'd brought it with me that Saturday when Dad and I went to visit his parents on their farm. Squirrel season had opened and I was hoping to ventilate a few of them with it in the farm's woodlot. Dad told me that Gramps had sold off some logs to a jobber and they might be working in the woodlot and could spoil my hunt.

They were and they did.

When we pulled into the farm there were two pickup trucks, a couple cars, a state police cruiser, and an ambulance parked off to the side of the night pasture where a bunch of logs were pushed into a pile. Dad pulled in next to them and we got out. Gram came walking with a distraught, yet sympathetic, look on her farm-worn face.

"You might want to keep the boy in the truck, Jim, or send him in the house. There's been an accident. Roscoe Barker's hired man got killed in the woodlot this morning by a widowmaker. They'll be bringing him out directly."

"Christ almighty!" my father swore, something he did rarely within earshot of his mother. "Who was it?"

"Flint Hagman. Lives over in Jonesville. Only twenty-two years old."

"What's a widow-maker, Dad?" I asked as Gram turned and walked away toward the house. I saw her take a handkerchief out of her apron pocket and dab at something on her face.

"It can be quite a few things when it comes to logging. Most generally it's a dead limb or a chunk of a tree leaning into another that's being cut and comes falling down on the logger because he doesn't see it in time. Makes a widow out of his wife. Logging's a dangerous business, son."

We could hear an engine puttering out of the woods and getting closer. Dad opened the tailgate of our pickup.

"You can stay. Sit here on the tailgate and don't speak unless you're spoken to," he said, and leaned against the fender.

A battered John Deere bulldozer came clattering out of the woods road, black smoke puffing out the exhaust pipe in rhythmic spasms. Behind the large dozer blade were a couple of eight-foot planks resting across the two push arms. A gray wool blanket covered a man-size lump lying on them, a pair of old clodhopper boots sticking out of one end. A silent cavalcade of followers marched behind the machine, all eyes cast downward.

Gramps walked over to Dad and me.

"What happened, Pa?"

"Flint was cutting down a big red oak near the south corner stone wall. He didn't see some vines going from the oak into an old beech way up in the tops. When the oak fell, the vines pulled a big dead chunk of the beech down on top of him."

As the bulldozer rumbled to a stop by the ambulance, a car pulled up and a young woman got out of the passenger side. It was the dead logger's wife. Even I could tell that she was well along in her pregnancy. She ran up and knelt by the blanket-draped body and started wailing in the most sorrowful cries I'd ever heard. Roscoe, the man driving the bulldozer, shut it off and climbed down. He walked around to the rear of it and sank to his knees, sobbing into his tattered Red Man hat. My dad turned to me and said, "Get in the truck, son. We need to leave and give these people some privacy."

We got into the truck and headed for home. Shooting squirrels suddenly seemed like such a thoughtless thing to do. There'd been enough death in the woods without me adding to it.

On the drive home I asked Dad if what happened to the logger was a common occurrence. He told me that it happened more often than a person would think. I remarked that he had a chainsaw and used it a lot to cut our firewood supply, as well as the wood for his parents' farmhouse, and he never got hurt.

"Yes, son, but I do it part time, as careful as I can. Working in the woods for a living is a hell of a hard way to support a family."

"I think being in the woods would be a great way to spend the day," I said.

"Don't even think about being a logger. What you want to do is find yourself a steady job with a good company with benefits and put in your time. Do what you want to do in your spare time, like I do."

My dad believed any idiot could run a chainsaw. He'd purchased a McCulloch 1-42 chainsaw in 1961 and swore by it and swore at it for the rest of his life. I still have it on a shelf in my barn. And now, after running a chainsaw for forty years, I'd say being an idiot is almost a requirement.

Consider this basic description of a chainsaw: It's a heavy, badly balanced collection of metal and plastic, gasoline and oil, shaking in your hands. A long, thin, metal blade called a *bar* is sticking out of it. A narrow loop of chain with razor-sharp teeth travels in a tiny groove in the edge of the bar and around a drive sprocket. The sprocket is turned by a gasoline engine. This drives the chain at eighty-five feet per second. Because the piston in the engine is going up and down two hundred times per second, if sharpened correctly, it will slice through a rock maple log easy as pie. Even a dull chain will cut through flesh like Jell-O. It'll lop off an arm or leg in a heartbeat. It's a marvelous tool in the right hands; an accident waiting to happen in the wrong ones.

I bought my first chainsaw when I was sixteen years old. My mom floated me the $250 I needed and set up a monthly payment plan. I felt I would easily make the payments, since I could make scads of money in the timber market I would soon have cornered. By my reasoning, money did grow on trees. I never factored into my financial figuring the glaring truth the young never see: I was so green, if you'd stuck me in the ground I would've grown. Thankfully, I also had another quality that comes with youth. I may have been short on experience, but I had a tremendous amount of enthusiasm.

My safety training with the chainsaw was brief and to the point: my dad told me to be careful. He'd trucked home some log-length firewood from a housing development where he was clearing the roads and house lots. He did this while he was resting from his real job as a mechanic running a bus garage. I made a deal with him to cut and split the firewood. If I blocked up and split the wood needed for our house, I could sell what was left. We figured we had twice as much wood as our needs required, so it worked out I did it on halves—half for him, half for me. And then there was the half-assed way I went about it. Off to the pile of logs I swaggered, with my chainsaw in my hand and dollar signs in my head.

I quickly discovered a chainsaw doesn't do you a whole lot of good if it isn't sharp. Dirt and mud on a log will dull the teeth on the chain within minutes. My chainsaw would be duller than a two-year hoe and cutting wood almost as fast. I had to learn how to sharpen my chain with a file, and that wasn't the breeze I'd thought it'd be. It takes patience, practice, and experience. Things that are in short supply for a teenager. But I gnawed through the logs like a beaver with a toothache and was able to make my payments on the loan.

It wasn't the quick, easy money I'd hoped for. But I thought I could earn more if I cut out the middleman. I figured if I harvested trees and did actual logging, I would be the next lumber baron of the state of Vermont. I'd be rolling in more dough than a baker's knuckles.

I knew I would need help for such a hefty undertaking, so I recruited my best buddy, Art, into the cause. Art was my best friend since turd grade when we had joined forces against the reign of terror cast on us by our teacher, Old Lady Assburn. Art was smart, dependable, loyal, brave, and a hard worker—veritable Boy Scout without the uniform and merit badges. He also had a connection through his church with the county forester, Bill Hall. It was damn close to divine intervention that got us our first log job.

Art and I met with Mr. Hall in his office and told him of our desire to work in the woods. All we asked for was a chance to prove ourselves. Then we'd be on our way to fame and fortune in the timber-harvesting industry. We were bitten bad by the logging bug, and Bill figured he had the antidote to cure our itch. He took us to an overgrown cow pasture full of white pine in Williston. It was the sorriest excuse for a log job in the tri-state area. Trees were growing thicker than hair on a boar's ass. Limbs on the trees started about six inches off the ground and went all the way to the tippity top. Scattered throughout the stand were trees marked to be cut with yellow paint.

There's an insect called the white pine weevil that eats the top terminal bud of pine trees. This woodlot had been their all-you-can-eat buffet. Every time they ate the top bud off, it put another crook in the tree. The few trees that were big enough for logs were crooked as a dog's hind leg. This made the trees marketable only as four-foot pulpwood, which is used to make paper, and worth a paltry $16 per cord stacked roadside. A cord of wood is a pile four feet wide by four feet tall by eight feet long. Also marked to cut were some huge old pasture pines that had been the seed trees for the younger, crooked, pecker poles. These monsters were about four feet in diameter with massive limbs shooting out in all directions starting a few feet from the ground. Once again, all pulpwood.

Mr. Hall told us the pulp mill had a twenty-four inch maximum diameter limit on the wood it would accept, so those butt pieces would be too big. We'd have to split the four-foot bolts by hand with wedges and a splitting maul to reduce them down to the twenty-four inch limit. He informed us the landowner got three dollars per cord out of the sixteen dollars for the pulp. For the cherry on top, the job had to be done in the winter, because there were wet spots that would have to be frozen for the ground to be workable.

Art and I called a business meeting. We decided to take the job immediately before somebody else snatched it up. Apparently, ambition beats brains.

It took Art some serious groveling and begging, but his dad, Ed, volunteered his 9N Ford Jubilee tractor as our means of skidding. Then he volunteered to drive it because he didn't trust us with his tractor. When winter blew in, we worked the job weekends and during school vacations. Ed taught Art how to drive the tractor and jumped ship. Art and I preferred that he was gone so we could implement our own method of logging, our primary technique being bulling and jamming, which means working like the devil using primarily main strength and ignorance.

There was one practice we found quite entertaining, Ed less so. The big old monster pasture pines had numerous, large limbs and huge crowns up top and were surrounded by lots of other trees. When I cut the massive brutes, they wouldn't fall to the ground. They would sort of lean over and get hung up on other trees. The old Jubilee didn't have enough balls to pull the tree down.

I found I could solve that dilemma by walking up the leaning tree and cutting the limbs off as I went. The entertaining part came when I would cut off a limb that was holding the tree up. This would cause it to drop down and usually roll one way or the other, sometimes just a few feet until it got hung up again. But if I cut the kingpin holding it lodged to another tree, it'd go all the way down and I'd get one hell of a ride. I had to cling to it and stay to the upper side while holding my running chainsaw. I'd perform a fair imitation of a 148-pound squirrel.

Somehow, we survived the winter and came out of it with a much clearer understanding of the timber harvesting trade. One would think poverty would be a powerful enticement for leaving the woods. It wasn't. I loved working in the woods. Much of my childhood had been spent roaming the forest around my home to the point where I felt like part of it. And now felling trees had caught my interest like nothing else before. There had to be a way to make money doing it, and I decided I'd keep at it until I found one. I hoped it'd be soon, because I had a chainsaw to pay for.

During the summer, I was hired to help clear a building lot and power line right-of-way for a neighbor. This honed my meager felling skills, as well as my ability to sharpen my chainsaw chain to a reasonable edge.

I'm smarter than your average bear, and by my senior year I'd soaked up oodles of wisdom and earned copious class credits. Therefore, I attended only morning classes the last semester. This left the afternoons open for gainful employment—employment that I found working for a logger named Kenny Cutright.

Kenny agreed to pay me two dollars and fifty cents per hour to cut down trees for him. In order to receive that top-dollar wage, I had to supply my own chainsaw, gas, and bar oil. (A chainsaw has a separate tank for this oil, which is used to lubricate the bar and chain.) This was so Kenny could hire me as a subcontractor and avoid any liability and workers' compensation insurance. He wisely pointed out that I probably wouldn't need it anyway.

Winter was brutal that year. Snow right up to my bellybutton and colder than a witch's elbow. By the end of the first week of work, I'd been frozen so much I was farting snowflakes. Running a chainsaw shook the blood right out of my hands, and they froze nearly solid. Luckily, they were frozen to my chainsaw handles and I could keep right on working.

It was the second week on the job, and I was starting to think I was pretty slick with a chainsaw. I'd felled a large hemlock tree over a ravine that was forty feet across and fifteen feet deep. The butt of the tree rested on one bank of the ravine; the top end lay over on the other.

Once a tree is down, the limbs are cut off, or *limbed-out*. Using the proven method I'd enjoyed on leaning trees, I began walking out on it and cutting the limbs off. Pretty soon I was halfway across the ravine with a sizeable air gap underneath me to the bottom. I tried to ignore it and kept cutting off limbs.

Unknown to me, when I had dropped the hemlock across the ravine, I had created what is known as a *spring pole*. The falling tree had bent over a small sapling underneath it and held it under intense pressure. I bent over and reached underneath the hemlock to cut a limb and inadvertently cut the spring pole. It was well named.

It shot out from underneath the hemlock like the arm of a catapult and hit me square in the jaw. Blew my pilot light right out. Chucked me off the tree and down into the snowy ravine. And that's where Kenny found me, led by the sound of my chainsaw still idling beside me in the snow. He rousted me from my nap and helped me out of the ravine and sat me on a stump while I waited for the woods to stop spinning.

"Maybe you ought to head out," he said as he brushed some of the snow off my back. "You're looking kind of frazzled."

I sat there and checked to see if my jaw still worked. I figured Kenny was wondering what sort of a logger he'd hired. But once my head cleared and my ears stopped ringing, I knew what sort. The sort that wouldn't tolerate quitting. The type whose parents had taught that achievement isn't always measured by what you get done, but by what you have to go through to get there.

"Well Kenny," I said, "If it's all the same to you, I'd rather stay. I'll work my way out of it." And by God I did. I worked out the day and the rest of the winter. All the way through until spring breakup when the frost leaves the ground and logging ends for a spell.

I finished the job with a deep, satisfying feeling of accomplishment and capability. I'd met the challenges of the winter woods with a chainsaw as my means of earning my wages. I took the first determined steps on the forested road that I would wobble up for the next forty years—a path that would teach me many lessons of life, the first being that getting knocked on my ass was one of the best ways to keep me on my toes.

Chapter 2
Getting the Maine Idea

When Art and I graduated from high school in June of 1975, our parents made it clear to us that our logging days were done. We were to be roommates at Vermont Technical College in the fall. I was taking agribusiness, and Art was learning civil engineering. Neither one of us was totally sold on our choice of study, but it sounded good and made our parents happy. But sometimes other forces come to bear. Simple, daily occurrences that shape one's life in outstanding and unseen ways.

It began one beautiful morning in late July following my graduation. My mom was walking down a slight incline on her way to the garden. There was dew on the grass, and she slipped and fell. It wasn't a hard fall. She got up and went about her chores.

Later that afternoon, she started to feel sick. By evening, she was in agony and Dad rushed her to the hospital. The doctors suspected the fall had loosened a blood clot. For the next week, they treated her with blood thinners. But she got worse. They finally discovered she had a ruptured spleen and performed emergency surgery. But because of all the blood thinners, they couldn't stop the bleeding. She was fifty-two years old and the mother of six kids. And I realized there was one, simple reason why my Mom had died: there was dew on the grass.

Dad never shed a tear. My older sister was with him in the waiting room when the doctor came and told him the love of his life, his wife for nigh onto thirty years, wouldn't be coming home to us. He just sat down, put his head in his hands and said, "How the hell am I going to tell the kids?"

Three days after her death was my eighteenth birthday—a date on the calendar that declared I was a grownup. I knew I'd gotten a three-day head start on it. Now I could vote, defend my country, drink a beer. Make my own choices.

When Art and I arrived at college the end of August, our friendship became indestructible. Bulletproof. Any rough edges got worn off. A trust and familiarity took hold. At the end of the semester, I received a 2.9, Art got a 2.8. Hell, a 3.0 gets you on the dean's list. We didn't flunk out. We were both raised to give our best to everything we did, even if we didn't like it.

And then we both quit. I quit, not because I couldn't do the work, but because I couldn't do the life: the life I saw down the path I was being shoved along. Sending me off to college was a clear, sensible way for my dad to address one part of his life: a life that had been turned upside-down. But he couldn't fix his life by arranging mine. Nor could I live my life to satisfy the wishes of my dead mother. I had to search for the life I wanted. A life that would bring me contentment and happiness in a place I belonged. I had to answer the summons I heard within me, and it was coming from the forest.

There're countless varieties of "dew on the grass" throughout life. It can show up in many places. I wouldn't live my life trying to avoid it. Art and I decided we weren't going to fritter away precious time in our lives doing something that didn't suit us. Agribusiness? I might make a living selling farm equipment, but I couldn't buy into it for life. And Art needed to be a civil engineer like a frog needed sideburns.

So we came up with a plan. Much to our parents' dismay, we enrolled in a vocational logging school in Maine. Lucky for us, it only takes six months to learn how to be a logger. Three of the six months were spent in a Georgia Pacific logging camp. We called it the Roaring Splinter.

Students were divided into three-man crews. Two cutters and a skidder driver. The skidder-driving job was rotated each day; the skidders were rotated each week. One week a crew would have a John Deere, the next week, a Timberjack, then a Franklin, or a Tree Farmer or Clark Ranger. We learned which brand of skidder tipped over the easiest and which ones took more effort. Some would pull a wicked good load; another couldn't pull the hat off your head. Some had steering wheels, others had just a lever to steer them. The designs were still being worked out.

With eleven students in our class, there had to be one, two-man crew. Art and I were it. Each week Georgia Pacific tallied up the wood to pay us. Each week Art and I cut more wood than the other three crews put together. We earned back our tuition.

Art and I were good workers, but in all fairness, our classmates didn't set the bar real high. If brains were sunshine, they were laying in the shade. One day we were learning how to drive skidders in a huge field with one big mother rock in it. Two guys got the skidder stuck on the rock. Another was too inept to turn the skidder around in the woods, so he'd back it all the way in from the landing, which is the clearing where the logs are brought roadside.

I lost count of how many chainsaws they destroyed. The most popular method was to run them over with a skidder, although felling a tree on them achieved reliable results too. This tends to curb production as well as tax the patience of the instructors. Art and I might have been the long-haired hippies from Vermont, but the top French Canadian loggers we shared the camp with developed a grudging respect for us. They knew we could make the sawdust fly and the wood hit the landing.

The only classmate worth his salt, and he became a good friend, was from Chazy *(shay-zee)*, New York. Pete was the craziest, wildest person I'd ever met. He was crazy from Chazy. He could party like a brain-damaged test monkey, a trait that allowed him to fit in perfect with Art and me.

Pete had a Plymouth Duster, and dust it he did. Pete was the only guy I'd ever met who always wore his seat belt and shoulder strap. And he made anybody in his car do the same. After riding with him for ten minutes, you'd understand why. We'd ride home with him occasionally, and he could turn that eight-hour ride into a white-knuckle-grip six. We didn't see much of him after we left the school in Maine. But he was a good friend who made an indelible mark on my life.

Chapter 3
Back Home in the Land of Eden

When we came home in the fall of '76, Art and I got a job cutting and bunching for a logger out of Middlebury by the name of Jim Rumney. He had a job in Starksboro that was mountain goat terrain. We had a bird's-eye view of the Champlain Valley from the steep mountainside we were working.

Cutting and bunching means felling the tree, limbing-out the tree, and cutting off the top or *top off* the part that won't make a log, then pulling, or *bunching*, the marketable portions to the main skid road using a small bulldozer equipped with a winch to hitch onto them. We used eight-foot-long chain chokers with a bitch hook on one end. The choker goes around the log and through the bitch hook. A link of the chain beyond the bitch hook is slid into a keyhole slider on the winch cable. Once there's enough bunched for a load, or *hitch*, the log skidder hitches onto them and skids, or *twitches*, them to the log landing. When there is enough for a *jag*, or load for the log truck, the trucker loads them up with his cherry picker and takes them to the sawmill.

Let me recap. Trees are cut, limbed out, and topped off, then bunched to the main skid road. The skidder hooks onto the chokers and twitches a hitch of logs out to the landing. The trucker loads them with his cherry picker and takes a jag to the mill.

The lingo of the logger wasn't taught in the course at the school. We learned it along the way. A very vigorous vernacular of cuss words is also used at appropriate points throughout the process of getting logs to the truck. In some cases, I believe it's mandatory. Maybe even state law. There might be loggers who don't use them. I have yet to meet one in Vermont.

I was the cutter and cut down the trees. Art drove the dozer and bunched them to the skid road for Jim to twitch out with a little C4 Tree Farmer skidder. We were each paid $30 a day. One track on the old Case 350 bulldozer Art drove had a worn, bent front idler sprocket. It would throw off the track if you farted while leaning the wrong way. When it came off, it was a pounding, prying, knuckle-skinning, finger pinching affair to get it back on. Not a plum assignment, but Dad always told me that life ain't all romance.

When Jim secured another woodlot to cut, up north in Richford, Art and I rented an apartment over Gilman's Ben Franklin Store in town. Jim acquired a big Caterpillar skidder and Art bunched with the C4 instead of the track-throwing Case. We learned a lot about logging working together that winter. Grew closer as a work team and friends. We had been roommates in college and at the logging school and now shared the apartment too. We were like family, living and logging together 24/7; helping each other out and backing each other up.

After our employment with Jim petered out at the spring mud season, we both moved back home to our parents' houses to regroup. Art took a job working construction, though he missed being in the woods. I landed a job with a logger in Jeffersonville who was working a large woodlot in Eden. His name was Glenn. He was a gangly old goober with wind scoops for ears and was so thin and tall he could hunt geese with a long rake. Glenn had been a logger all his life, as was his father before him. And his before that. He paid me by the tree: eighty cents per tree. And once again, I had to supply my chainsaw, gas, and bar oil, allowing him to hire me as a subcontractor and avoid any workers' compensation insurance. I was starting to see a pattern here.

The first day I went to work for Glenn, he came into the woods to see what I could do. Glenn watched from a few yards away as I began to drop a fair-sized maple. I was a bit nervous with him eyeballing my performance. As the maple started to fall, I was trying to finish my hinge wood on the far side of my back cut. My chainsaw was buried to the hilt in the tree, and as it started to fall, it hit another tree on the edge of the opening in the forest canopy I was trying to thread it through. This caused the tree to break its hinge wood, twist on the stump, and roll into the opening. My chainsaw got pinched in the cut and twisted with the tree. When the tree trunk came off the stump, it put a 90-degree bend right in the middle of my chainsaw bar. Well lick my leg!

Glenn was some impressed. "Young feller, ya shouldn't have your saw buried in the cut like that when ya finish it. I see it right off."

This would be one of the many nuggets of wisdom I gleaned from Glenn over the length of my employ. He gave me the job, though, and even lent me one of his chainsaws to finish out the day, which I thought quite sporting of him, considering my recent demonstration of my prowess with a chainsaw. I sure showed him what I could do!

Glenn's skidder driver's name was Pinto. He came to work quite reliably, as he had to ride with Glenn because he'd lost his license to numerous DWI infractions. He once saw a sign that said, "Drink Canada Dry," and he headed north and gave it his best.

Johnny was the bulldozer driver or buncher. He was a square-headed, sawed-off fellow who ran everything full throttle: chainsaw, bulldozer, or skidder. He talked fast, as though he was taking bids at a farm auction. He could do about ten words a second, with gusts to fifty. He chewed tobacco pretty much nonstop. This could lead to serious spackling during the conversation if you didn't keep your distance. I was about a week into the job when Pinto came in one Monday morning to get his paycheck and drive skidder while he recuperated from his weekend bender. Glenn always paid on Monday. He said it was the best way to get the crew to show up.

Johnny and I sat on the front hood of the skidder and rested our feet on its decking blade each morning for the ride up the mountain to where we were cutting and bunching. We pulled our feet up out of the way when Pinto raised the blade. When it stopped, we set them down on it. On this occasion, Pinto, in his Monday morning stupor, had stopped a couple inches short of fully raising the decking blade. We thought he was done and put our feet down on it. But as he stomped down on the foot feed and tore off up the mountain, he finally raised it the last little bit.

This got my immediate attention because my left heel was caught and crushed between the blade and the front radiator grill of the skidder. Ouchee-wa-wa! Trying to make my predicament heard over the scream of a Detroit Diesel engine at full blast wasn't bringing the results I was craving for.

I quickly resorted to pounding on Johnny's leg next to me to see if he could possibly get Pinto to lower the blade a tad. I felt it would be beneficial if I could extract what was left of my heel. Pinto finally realized something was amiss and lowered the blade and stopped the skidder. Johnny and I slid to the ground roadside as Pinto climbed off the skidder. I proceeded to limp and hop around swearing fluidly and with vigor, while slyly working in the words moron and blade where needed.

"Christ almighty!" Johnny yelled, "I think I swallered my chew! You about broke my leg pounding on me! Hell, you're limping around like you was caught in a bear trap. Your foot broke much?" Like being broke just a little would be okay.

"I don't know if its broke or not!" Son of a bitch my heel hurt! I turned to Pinto.

"Why the hell did you pull the blade up that last little bit? We had our feet on it!"

"I thought I had it all the way up. I was checking to make sure. How was I to know your heel was there. You want to head home? How bad you hurt?" Pinto wasn't apologetic and didn't give two hoots in hell if we worked or not.

"Give me a minute. Let me walk it off."

I paced back and forth, putting most of my weight on the ball of my foot. I could walk. Hurt like hell, but I could walk. I was a week into the job. Glenn gave me this chance, even after my demonstration on bar bending.

"Let's go. I'll work out of it."

As a matter of record, I worked the day through and the following two weeks. I finally decided something was wrong in my left foot because of the constant, severe shooting pain. When I limped to the doctor, the X-ray showed a chunk of bone was busted off my heel.

"By the look of the swelling and discoloration, I'd say this happened a while ago," said old Doc Evans.

"Yeah, it was a couple of weeks ago," I confessed.

"Why the hell did you wait so long to see me?" Doc asked with raised eyebrows.

"Well, Doc, I figured I'd try to work my way out of it."

He applied a plaster cast from my toes to my knee. Said he should put one on my head, too, but he didn't think it would cure what was ailing it. Then he told me I needed to be on crutches for two weeks, and the cast had to remain on for a month. It was quite cumbersome and itched to beat three of a kind. After two weeks, I sawed that sucker off and went back to bulling. Glenn wasn't going to wait forever. Working out of it had always cured me in the past. I figured I just didn't give it a fair shake. And I was right. It healed up fine.

Once I got back to work, I tried to convinced Glenn that he needed to hire Art. I'd been singing Art's praises ever since Johnny quit. Johnny had left his job as dozer driver for a different occupation—one where he figured he had a better chance of surviving—leaving Glenn short one buncher.

For a while, Glenn had Crazy George, the log bucker on the landing, fill in for Johnny. Crazy George had earned that moniker during numerous stints in the Waterbury nuthouse over the course of his life. I never knew his last name or his age. Nor did I ever call him Crazy George to his face because, like Johnny, I wanted to get home alive.

Crazy George was probably around 60. Working with him was like working next to a keg of dynamite with a wet fuse. You knew he was going to go off, but you didn't know when. Glenn had kept him bucking trees into logs on the landing. But this meant he had an ax or a chainsaw in his hands. If you pissed him off, it wasn't out of character for him to chase after you with that four-pound tomahawk. I remember coming to work one morning and getting out of my car to hear a loud banging noise.

It was Crazy George. He had his ax and was pounding on the apron of the skidder and screaming incoherently.

Glenn was happy to send him off into the woods with me, as he was tired of trying to outrun him on the landing. George might have been sixty, but it was a spry sixty. In the woods, George would bunch trees with the bulldozer and yell at me for being a college-educated logger who didn't know squat about cutting trees. To keep the peace, I'd pretend to agree with him.

One day I had a large, heavily leaning white ash marked to cut. I studied it for some time trying to figure out how in the Sam Hill I was going to cut it down without splitting it from stump to crown. I might've not known much about cutting trees, but I did know white ash is straight grained and splits wicked easy. And a heavy lean only provokes this tendency. If I couldn't make the back cut fast enough, or if I left too much hinge wood as it fell, it would split the tree. Or as we loggers call it, barber-chair. That would ruin the log. And just to keep things interesting, the half that splits toward the cutter can ruin his day when it takes his head off. Crazy George watched me survey the tree, and he started cussing at me for pussy-footing around and wasting time and losing him money.

"George," I said "if you would like to educate me and show me how to cut this here tree proper, I'd sure like to see it. They never taught me how to do it right in logger college."

It was all the prodding he needed. He jumped off the dozer and grabbed my chainsaw. He never would wear a hard hat. I think the few brain cells he had needed all the air they could get. He fired up my saw, adjusted his baseball cap, stepped up to that massive ash, and began gnawing at it like a hungry beaver.

When the tree started to fall, it split and barber-chaired. Thirty feet of it split, and half of it shot 20 feet into the air with a report like a rifle. It took the baseball cap clean off Crazy George's head and didn't even muss his hair.

I stood there with my mouth open and my eyes bugged out like a stepped-on toad. Crazy George walked over, picked up his hat, and screwed it back on his cranium. He handed me my chainsaw, started bitching about losing his eighty cents on the ash, and told me to get my ass back to work so we could make up the deficit.

I pulled Glenn aside at the end of the day and told him what happened. I also told him I'd rather shave my ass with a cheese grater than work another day with Crazy George. He agreed to hire Art. He had to supply the cable and chokers for the bulldozer so Glenn could hire him as a subcontractor and pay him eighty cents a tree, too, liability insurance being a frill we couldn't afford. We probably wouldn't need it anyway.

Chapter 4
The Art of Work

Working with my best friend instead of Crazy George was like going to heaven. When getting paid by the tree, it's to the advantage of both the cutter and the dozer operator to work as a team. Payment isn't earned until the trees get bunched to the skid road for counting. The cutter shouldn't just lay trees down willy-nilly and make the dozer driver fight through the mess to bunch them. The two need to plan together how they're going to get the trees from stump to skid road.

On the steep, rocky terrain of Vermont, there may well be only one way to get into an area to get the timber out. Savvy loggers won't screw up their only chance by going at it ass-backwards. Then there's the added burden of deep ravines, boulders, rocks, cliffs, brooks, swales, and swamps, plus a couple of feet of snow for months at a time.

And that's just some of the terrain challenges. Black flies, mosquitoes, no-see-ums, and swarms of deer flies attack unceasingly during the spring and summer. I don't know what they live on when they can't get loggers. Wasp, hornet, and yellow jacket nests are often found the hard way. Nothing gets a guy's attention quicker than a huge white-faced hornet caught under his hard hat. Steamy summer days can make the landing like a little tin hell with a lid on it. Driving rain, gale force winds and blanketing snowstorms pound the woods throughout the seasons. It's like wiping your ass on a wagon wheel: there ain't no end to it.

The days we can work are days we need to make the fur fly. To do so, the cutter, by using his skill in directional felling techniques, can make the bunching of trees a hell of a lot easier. And quite frequently, if we could drive the bulldozer up to the tree, we would use the hydraulic, all angle blade on it to push trees in the desired direction.

It's a mistake to drop the trees in whatever direction nature leaned them if it makes it more difficult to remove them. All trees have a natural lean. Indeed, a whole ridge of timber can have the same natural lean brought on by the prevailing winds as they grew. It won't be a hundred percent, but damn close. Consideration needs to be taken about how and where the crew will get equipment in to get the timber out.

Many times, we used existing old roads for skidding and bunching. It paid to seek these out. It might be only a four- or five-foot-wide old horse trace we had to piece together, but nine times out of ten, the old boys who were there before had found the best, and sometimes the only place to access a certain ridge or swamp.

Other times, we had to put in new roads. Either way, it's well worth spending time to canvas or "cruise" the area to be logged. By knowing which direction the trees lean and where the roads access an area will help determine where to begin cutting. I've learned to use any slight advantage possible since it might save a lot of time and trouble down the road. When cutting large timber on rough terrain, it pays to meet trouble halfway and head it off, because I've learned that trouble is quite capable of making the full journey all by itself.

Accidents happen right out of the blue. On one occasion, I'd just turned off my chainsaw and was walking from one tree to the next. It was summer, and I was wearing a T-shirt. My feet slipped in the dry leaves on the steep hillside. The chainsaw rotated in my grasp when the bar tip hit the ground behind me. It pushed the blazing hot muffler of the chainsaw against the back of my forearm. I could hear the sizzle of sweat and smell the burning flesh. I fell, slid, screamed, and stood up. In three seconds, I'd been branded like a steer. Made my eyes water up. This happened about nine o'clock in the morning. I worked my way out of it.

My point is that even though safety is forefront in your mind, dangerous things can happen with no warning. Do you believe in fate? Do you believe in luck? Do you believe events are preordained? I've seen things in my forty years in the woods that tell me all three are possible. Providence doesn't fire any blank cartridges. I know if a tree falls in the forest, it may not make a sound, but it may damn well kill me.

Even trees that have long since fallen can be a danger lying in wait. A job Art and I worked up in Sheldon brings to mind a mishap I'd rather forget. The scabs were just peeling off my fried forearm when I had another fun-filled episode.

This woodlot had many shelves and ridges and contained a

lot of rock ledges. I had to cut a large white birch a dozen feet back from a five-foot-high ledge running parallel to the hillside we were working on. To facilitate bunching it to the skid road, I decided to lay it diagonally across and over the ledge.

In my eagerness to earn my eighty cents, I didn't consider an old pine that was blown down. It was lying on the ground up hill from me and the birch. It ran out in the same general direction I had chosen to fell the birch. I thought it would snap off the top half of the rotten old pine hanging over the ledge. It did not. When I dropped the birch onto the pine, it threw it, root ball and all, downhill over the ledge. And I was right in its way!

I was turning to run when it hit my thigh and threw me over the five-foot ledge and down the steep hillside. I dropped my chainsaw and got one hand down on top of the ledge, sort of like a cartwheel, before I went over it. But my right index finger landed in a crack in the ledge and stuck there just long enough to dislocate it. I landed on my feet on the downhill side but had to tuck and roll, both from my momentum and to avoid the pine. A one-man avalanche.

Art saw my performance and, being quite impressed, awarded me a score of 9.2. He took off points because I didn't stick the landing. My finger looked like a gnarled-up piece of ginger root. Smarted a might too. Art grabbed on to it as I braced myself on a tree and he jerked it back into the socket while I screamed like a goosed soprano.

Thank God it happened late on a Friday afternoon, because my finger swelled up to the size of a kielbasa. The right-hand index finger runs the throttle on a chainsaw, and this proved quite painful for the coming week.

Art and I were starting to hit our stride. We got better and smarter at cutting and bunching. We were averaging seventy-five trees a day. One day we hit 110. We were earning nigh onto $300 a week and having a picnic lunch to boot.

It might not sound like much money nowadays. But back in 1977 the minimum wage was two-twenty an hour or eighty-eight dollars per week. We were twenty years old and living life for all it was worth, in the best shape we would ever be. Blue twisted steel. We were what men of the woods called *cordy*: had the stamina of a good plow horse and not enough fat on either one of us to grease a skillet.

Photo courtesy of VFF

To cut and bunch seventy-five trees a day, we had to hustle. We learned how to save steps, figured out how to do things faster, easier, better. One day we'd be in a poor chance, some nasty hole of a spot, and bust our humps to get forty-five trees bunched in a long day. We'd bull and jam our way out of it and come into a good chance with nice timber, and the next day have sixty trees by noon. The pendulum swung back and forth. We covered ground. Our teamwork attack was really gelling. We started to know what the other guy was going to do before he did it.

A trust develops when two men work side by side, day after day, dealing with deadly forces. They learn to work with a heads-up attitude, not just for themselves, but for their co-worker too. And in this case, their best friend.

I kept my eyes open and my mind working. Is that a dead limb in the forest canopy? Does Art see it? Is that dead tree (or what is called a *stub*) leaning this way? Did I weaken it when I dropped that tree? When I cut the top off this tree, is it going to roll? And if so, where? Is Art in danger trying to hook onto it as I top it? This is how that inner voice speaks if you want to get through the day still breathing. Making a living along the way becomes secondary.

There came a sticky summer day, hotter than two rats screwing in a wool sock. Art and I were on a mountain in Eden, working on a fifty-yard-wide flat spot on the side of it—what we called a shelf. I'd gone up the mountainside and dropped a tree downhill toward the shelf, limbed it out, and topped it off. Trees to be cut had been marked by spots of blue paint by the forester. I was still up the hill a bit when I saw another tree close by on the sidehill, marked with two spots of blue paint, which meant I had to girdle it, not cut it down.

To girdle a tree means I use my chainsaw and make a waist-high cut all the way around the circumference of the tree, about two inches deep, until the cut meets. This kills the tree slowly, but leaves it standing. It'll become what is known as a den tree—food for woodpeckers and nesting cavities for mice, birds, squirrels, and others. I got paid ten cents a tree for girdling. I made my way over to it. It was a big, tight-barked beech. I girdled it and headed on downhill.

I cut down another tree, and was moving along it, cutting branches off. I had on ear protection and my chainsaw was screaming like a banshee. Art was behind me about twenty-five feet away, pulling winch cable to the tree I was working on. Without warning, I was blind-sided by Art as he grabbed me in a running tackle. All I could think was, "What in the hell is he doing, grabbing me while I'm running my chainsaw?!" I dropped the saw as he took me down. He held me in a bear hug and kept us rolling along the ground. The top-most branches of that girdled beech slapped across our ankles as it pounded to the forest floor behind us.

We stood up, side by side, and looked at the massive tree lying there where I had just been working. I said, "Holy shit, Art! That would've killed me. You saved my life, man!"

We turned and looked in each other's eyes. He put his hand on my shoulder and said, "Hell, Willy, you'd have done the same for me."

Looking back at him, I hoped to hell he was right. Nobody really knows how they'll react when mortal danger is stampeding at them and a life hangs in the balance of a few seconds. Art knew.

We walked up to the base of the beech. It was just as hollow as a politician's promise. When I'd girdled it, I'd cut just about everything that was keeping it standing. We never really talked about that day again. But I realized I came within a hair's breadth of being carried out on the blade of the dozer covered by a blanket.

Pinto saw it all happen as he drove up to get a hitch. He watched that man-killer beech drop down on us as we worked. He closed his eyes and turned his head. He didn't want to see us die. When he opened them after he heard the tree hit the ground and saw us pop up on the far side, he bailed off the skidder and ran over. He was school's-out happy to see us still kicking.

Chapter 5
Sustainable Logging

The first and foremost concern at that time in my logging career, besides staying in one piece, was to get the wood out to the log landing to make money. Sustainable logging meant sustaining a steady flow of timber. That holds true for most of today's loggers, too, if they're honest about it. The need to have a steady cash flow trumps almost any other card. Without it, you won't be logging for long. New equipment is expensive. Payments are high. Older iron is cheaper, but breakdowns will be more frequent. And lost production means lost money. Insurance premiums on equipment are steep because of the dangerous work. Workers' compensation rates are sky-high, sometimes unaffordable, so subcontracting is stretched beyond the imagination. Corners get cut. Priorities get adjusted.

Often, directional felling with wedges and pushing trees over with the blade of the bulldozer was done more to facilitate quick removal of the tree than to minimize damage to the woods. Sometimes I would be struggling to get a hitch and had to make a quick choice: Do I drop a tree in a direction that allows us to bunch it quickly but smashes a nice stand of rock maple saplings? Or do I spend extra time and labor wedging it over into some scurvy hardhack, wrestle with it, and take twice as long? Well, down into the rock maple it would go. And that's a sad fact, but when the skidder came to get a hitch, we had to have one bunched and ready or we'd be out of a job.

Glenn and Pinto would push us on purpose. Once Art and I were in a good chance and had 20 trees bunched by our nine o'clock break. We figured we had a good two hitches and could catch our breath. Pinto had several twelve-foot-long chain chokers on the skidder. By finagling and rehooking, he wrapped two or three trees in each choker and took all twenty. It was one of the biggest loads I'd ever seen a skidder pull. He laughed and hollered at us to get cracking because he'd be right back.

Another consideration was whose land we were on. If it was the mill owner's we worked for, his forester was involved. Care was taken to cut only trees marked and save the young growing stock. If it was land on which the stumpage—the value of the trees paid to the landowner—was lump sum–bought and we were doing a diameter cut, look out.

A diameter cut meant removing trees that were a certain diameter at breast height (DBH) and larger, usually twelve inches. This meant every tree that had an eight-foot log or longer, and was ten inches at the top end, was fair game. When we finished cutting in some areas, the woodpeckers had to lug their lunch in.

This wasn't logging for the faint of heart. There would be times when we'd churn and paw our way up mountainsides on the massive Clark Ranger skidder Glenn owned. It had chains on all four tires and would dig up the roads like a huge rototiller.

Brooks that were crossed on the way down with a hitch of logs might turn and follow the ruts and change the road into a river of mud. There was usually rock and hard pan just below the shallow topsoil on most woodlots we were on. Once the skidder tires dug down to it, they would scratch their way back and forth on that.

I recall a steep old road in Eden that gave us trouble. The topsoil was deep and the hard pan was too far down. The skidder was getting hung up on its belly pan. There was a brook near the top of this quarter-mile length of road, and on a Friday afternoon, with a weekend forecast for rain, Glenn had us turn the brook down the road with the bulldozer.

It rained like a cow pissing on a flat rock all weekend. When we arrived on Monday, the pond of mud at the bottom of the road was spectacular. Art spent an hour with the bulldozer pushing it off to the side of the road on a corner while I cut a hitch. He damn near got it buried. He had to hitch onto a tree behind him. He'd push mud and play out the winch cable. Push as far as he could, then winch himself back out. Later, when we rode on the skidder up that section, the banks of the road were almost even with the height of the hood of the skidder we sat on, about six feet.

It was during one of those rides, as I looked at the banks at eye level, that I began to question what I was a part of. It was such a blatant abuse of the woods I loved. A total lack of respect for the land that gave me my means of making a living and so much more. If this was an acceptable practice, then logging ethics were, indeed, on a slippery slope.

I didn't want to be in a street fight with the forest—a fight without rules of fair play—where equipment payments and contract deadlines, and sometimes greed, can take priority over treating the land with care and consideration. But I needed a job. And I needed to stay in the woods like a fish needs to stay in the water. I was learning more each day about cutting and skidding timber. By the sheer volume of trees I was cutting, I was getting better. There are certain things that you can only learn by doing. It's like learning how to track a buck. Tips from a master and studying on it help, but you must follow the buck, read the sign, and slay him on your own.

Chapter 6
The Chainsaw

As stated before, a chainsaw is a marvelous tool in the right hands. But only when sharpened correctly. And believe it when I say a sharp saw is safer than a dull one. A sharp chainsaw that feeds into the wood of its own weight in a nice straight line is what every cutter wants. Keeping a saw doing so takes skill with a file and knowledge of the nature of chainsaw teeth when applied to wood—hardwood and softwood, meaning, dense, deciduous, leafy trees or needled, porous, coniferous trees. And thawed wood and frozen wood.

A man who pushes on a dull saw to make it cut is going to get tired, and a tired logger is prone to accidents. It ain't the bullet that kills you, it's the hole. It's not the chainsaw that kills you, it's the teeth whizzing around the blade at eight-five feet per second as it takes a three-eighths-inch-wide chunk out of a leg, arm, or face. If the tip of the saw bar hits an unseen obstacle and it kicks back, there's a slim chance that it can be kept in control. Fatigue near the end of the day has laid more than one logger in the hospital. Or the morgue.

A fast-cutting chainsaw is needed when felling big hardwood timber. I always used a twenty-inch saw bar. It would allow me to cut just about any size tree I'd run across, up to forty inches. Even more if I reached into my felling notch and cut a little in there. I learned to do that the way I learned a lot about logging: trial and error, error being the operative word.

We'd moved back to the Eden woodlot. It was three thousand acres. You never really finish cutting on a lot that size, you just keep pecking away at it. Eden was where Glenn would go if he didn't have more profitable work.

We were a couple wagon races up the mountain on some very steep terrain. There was a lot of exposed ledge as we neared the top. Glenn pointed out a monster of a yellow birch up on a wicked steep hillside above where we stood. The crown was near dead and chunks were broken off it. What was left looked more like a dead stub than a solid tree.

"Make sure you cut that old birch up there," he said, pointing out the old monarch.

"You think it's any good?" I asked.

"I'll bet you it's solid and just as red as a fox's tail inside. You cut it and we'll find out." He walked down the skid road following Pinto driving out a hitch.

I climbed up to the birch and eyeballed it. It was a huge tree. Not real tall, as it was so high on the mountain its height was stunted by the altitude, but it's girth was substantial. I'd guess more than four feet at the stump where I'd be cutting it. There wasn't much for footing because it was so steep and rocky. I pawed and stomped some footholds in the little bit of duff and debris around it in the area I needed to stand to work. I cut a felling notch out of the downhill face, as that was the only direction this behemoth was going. I knew my chainsaw's bar might come up short of what I needed in order to cut my hinge wood to the proper width. But then I thought, "This tree is probably rotten in the middle. The center hinge wood won't amount to a fart in a whirlwind. I'll be lucky if it doesn't start falling before I'm halfway through the back cut."

And I thought wrong. I was watching my sawdust because it can tell a person if the tree being cut is solid or not. I could see dark red shavings, not mealy dust, even when I had the saw cutting in the center. Or at least as far into the center as my twenty-inch bar would allow. The tree was solid. When I came around to my side of the back cut, with my saw buried to the hilt and screaming full throttle, the old birch started to go. I'd cut all I could reach and knew it was time to leave. I turned to scramble sideways along the bank to get away, and I paused to look back.

I hadn't cut enough of the hinge wood! It was holding too much! Any other species of tree would've barber-chaired, but not this mountain-tough, stringy old yellow birch. The whole weight of it was hanging on the steep downhill side of the shallow-rooted tree, growing on ledge. The huge thirty-five-foot-diameter root ball of the birch came rising up out of the ground, starting on the uphill side, as the whole shooting match started pitching down off the mountain. With me on it!

The last thing a logger will do is abandon his chainsaw. They cost a considerable amount of money. And regardless of what some might claim, we also become sentimentally attached to them. A smooth running, easy starting, low-maintenance chainsaw becomes a loyal friend. It takes a matter of grave consequences to make a guy cut and run on his saw.

But I was in trouble. Two-handed trouble. I dropped Old Blister and made a leaping dive off the root ball as things became vertical. I wasn't sure what I was diving for, but I figured anywhere else would be a darn sight better than where I was.

Luck was with me. I just barely cleared a jagged chunk of rock and landed stretched out on my left side on the steep mountain and rolled down the near vertical sidehill, clawing for anything I could. My left hand grasped a two-inch beech sapling like a rung on the monkey bars. My grip held. My body swung downhill as rocks and debris bounced over me. Something took my hard hat off. I could feel the ground shaking.

The old birch churned its way down the hill for a hundred feet, taking everything in the way along for the ride. My shirt was ripped on my left side and I had a nasty scratch down those ribs. They would turn different colors over the next week from the pounding. My left knee was throbbing, but still worked.

When I realized I was sound and able, I went looking for my chainsaw. I could still hear it running. It'd landed in a little nook down under the huge root ball of the birch. She was there waiting for me, purring like a cat by a warm stove. I snaked my way in and pulled her out and shut her off.

Art came back from bunching a couple trees and pulled up alongside me where I sat on a stump, thanking my lucky stars. He shut the dozer off.

"What the hell, Willy?" he said as he surveyed the torn-up mountainside in front of him. I filled him in on what happened, hitting all the high points. He said he was sorry he missed my demonstration on root-ball riding. We had more dangerous work ahead of us to get the tree bunched. Cutting the birch the rest of the way off the stump was a ticklish job. To reach it, I had to stand on the nose of the crawler with that huge root ball looming over me. The birch was so big, the eight-foot choker Art used wasn't long enough to go around it. He had to use two, tied together. I cut what I dared to on the birch, and Art was able to bust the rest when he yanked on it with the winch. As he finally pulled it up behind the dozer to bunch it, I couldn't help but notice that the old tree was sound as a dollar and just as red as a fox's tail. The next few days were tough. I was so bruised up and lame I couldn't fart without crying. Deep breaths were painful. I worked my way out of it.

Chapter 7
Bulldozer Bunching

Bunching trees in the hills of Vermont with a small, woods-equipped bulldozer is an art form. And Art was just the man to do it. Some of the places he put that John Deere 450C crawler would flat out scare you. Worse would be some of the spots where he would pitch down over with a hitch of logs behind him.

Now when I say woods-equipped, I mean some protection on the rig. First off, a good canopy that can take a rollover or a tree pounding on it. I think that speaks for itself. You best have a rugged belly pan underneath it too. They're also called skid pans, because sometimes you'll be sliding over rocks and stumps on it. Without it, all kinds of things would be torn off and staved in under there—filters, hoses, housings.

It needs a pair of limb risers with a good, shielded exhaust pipe running alongside one of them to blow exhaust from the engine up over the cab. Limb risers are sturdy pipes that go from the front nose of the crawler up to the top of the canopy. Any limbs encountered by the dozer as it travels along will be pushed up over the cab instead of slapping you upside the head. You still have to pay attention because it doesn't stop them all. And nothing wakes you up quicker and sets the tone for the day better than getting bitch-slapped by a nasty little beech whip first thing in the morning.

The winch on the back of the dozer was a beast all its own. It could get you out of a jam and bunch timber better than a team of horses. Art kept three, eight-foot-long choker chains made of three-eighths-inch steel hanging on the back of the dozer above the winch. He would have a hundred feet of five-eighths-inch cable on the winch drum with three keyhole sliders for the choker chains. The winch could break either one if you weren't paying attention. That meant having to watch what you're winching and listen to the dozer motor. It'll lug down a bit if it hangs up on something. If you're ready on the winch control lever, you can stop it before it snaps and comes flying back at you like a rocket.

Keeping the cable from snarling up on the winch drum is a constant job that takes skill, patience, and practice. Sometimes, when winching in stems for long distances on sidehills, the cable will hog-up on one side of the drum. Not good. The operator must plan ahead to repeatedly shift the ass end of the dozer as the cable is being winched in so it fills the drum more evenly. It doesn't have to be perfectly spooled on. Wait until you're on better ground, or when the hitch is bunched, then drive ahead and play out the cable so it can be winched in again and a better job done. This is the secret to long cable life.

It's the first six feet, where the slides are always working, that takes a beating. Over time, it will develop wire hairs sticking off it that will pierce mittens, gloves, and hide, especially if your hands slip on it. Art would milk it for as long as he could tolerate, but eventually the first, hairiest few feet are cut off and a new knot tied. A nasty, dangerous job. It involves a cable cutter, a sledgehammer, vise grips, hopefully two guys, gritted teeth, and a fair amount of cussing.

The tracks of the bulldozer are what gets it through the woods. What sort of shape they're in determines where it can go. On frozen ground, the dozer needs to have the grouser pads (the steel plates that are bolted to the chain of the track) *calked*. Pronounced "corked," it's the equipment equivalent of putting spikes in your boots like the river loggers of old. Every fall we would have one-by-two-inch pieces of hardened steel grouser rod welded to the grouser edge of each pad. We put two pieces on each side of a pad and one in the middle of the next pad and repeated the process for the length of both tracks. These dig in to push and pull the dozer back and forth on frozen ground and packed snow. More importantly, they keep it from sliding sideways when going across a grade.

Sliding down a hill sideways in a bulldozer is a good way to get killed. When it finally hogs into something, be it a rock or stump or just some soft ground, there's a good chance it'll roll. With no seat belt on, your choices are to hold on and stay in it or jump out to the high side. Both suck a hind tit. If you're lucky, a tree stops it and keeps it from flipping. Understand, there were seat belts on the dozer. Art tucked them under the seat cushion. He would be off and on the crawler hundreds of times a day. Belting up each time just wasn't practical.

By the end of the winter, the calking would be worn down somewhat. The dozer would have wicked good traction with them on dry ground. Art had to be careful not to turn too tightly on ledge or tree roots, as it could tear the transmission or final drives out of the crawler because they gripped so well. By the next winter, they would be worn down even more, with some broken off, and they would have to be calked again.

The bulldozer had a hydraulically controlled blade on the front that could be moved six ways by a T-stick control lever. The blade could be lifted up and down, angled forward and back, and tilted side to side. With it we could move most rocks and cut into sidehills to make skid roads that we bunched to. It wouldn't remove big tree stumps, but up to about a ten-inch-diameter stump was no problem.

If there were bigger trees that had to be stumped out, we'd push the whole tree over, root ball and all, which is the quickest way to stump most trees, even the smaller ones. The bigger trees we got toppled over by scratching around the tree with the dozer blade and breaking off what roots it could. Then we pulled the dozer alongside the tree, stood on the canopy, and put a choker chain around the tree as far up as we could reach. Next, we attached the choker to the winch cable and played out a good length of cable. The leverage we gained by hooking high up on the tree made it fairly easy to winch the tree over.

Care had to be taken not to winch it over on top of the dozer. The technique was to get the tree coming over, then scoot the dozer out of the way by going perpendicular to its direction of fall, an operation that usually gets the heart pounding. It's not something you could practice. You either got it right or got a tree on you, and prayed the steel canopy held and you didn't get speared by a limb coming into the cab.

Running a bulldozer all day bunching trees is a taxing job. It isn't just sitting your ass on a piece of equipment. Even the sitting part will jar the soup right out of you. There's no suspension system on a crawler. You feel every bump and get thrown all around. Almost more time is spent looking back at the trees you're pulling than looking forward in the direction you're going. This can put a crick in a neck like no other.

The adjustment of the brake bands on the winch need to be set just right. They must be tight enough to hold the hitch while you're dragging the trees, but they also need to be set so the winch will free-spool sufficiently when the brake is released. This allows the cable to be pulled out easily when it is set in the free-spool position. But it can't be too easy! It needs enough resistance to keep the drum from spinning after you stop pulling. Otherwise, the cable on the drum will get snarled up like line on a big fishing reel.

Pulling sixty or seventy feet of five-eighths-inch cable uphill with a couple eight-foot choker chains draped over your shoulder will build muscle and character. Doing so in a foot or two of snow will put muscle in your shit. And the more cable that's out, the harder it pulls the part that's always on the drum—not only because of the sheer weight, but because the cable that doesn't get used a lot starts to take on the circular shape of the drum. It's similar to a coil spring that's trying to be stretched out. It'll even shoot back toward the bulldozer, especially if it's been pulled uphill. It needs to be draped around a tree or sapling or knelt on while hooking the choker around the log. A real tough logger will grip it with his teeth or pinch it between his butt cheeks.

Keeping the dozer tracks clean of mud is something that must be done daily, year-round. To that end, a short-handled fire spade was bungeed to the back of the dozer canopy, behind the chokers. At the end of the day, the last thing to be done was to shovel out any debris around the drive and idler sprockets of the tracks. When freezing weather was in the forecast, which could be six months of the year, this was paramount. Mud could freeze in there like concrete during the night and possibly break the final drive when the dozer was moved in the morning.

A smart operator would always park the crawler on some woody debris or a treetop to keep it from freezing to the ground. Using down pressure on the blade first thing in the morning to lift the front end of the dozer and break the tracks free was just common sense. And for God's sake, don't set the parking brake when leaving it for the night or weekend in cold weather! You might find it froze up tighter than a frog's ass when you come back and the dozer won't budge.

Having the ability to set a good, sturdy parking brake is necessary when bunching with a crawler, not for when you're winching in logs, but for when you get off the dozer on uneven ground to set and unhook chokers and pull cable. The parking brake on the John Deere 450C had a little, iron flip toggle down by your right foot, in the floor next to the foot brake. To engage it, the operator has to reach down by his heel and flip the toggle over and push down on the pedal. To release it, he has to mash down hard on the pedal while reaching down and flipping it back. It's the end point of the toggle, physically sticking into teeth along the edge of the brake pedal, that holds the pedal down. For obvious reasons, it can't be trusted. If it slips out of the tooth you've jammed it in, off she goes. If you bump it while climbing on the dozer and sitting down, be ready for a ride.

We used it, but we rarely trusted it completely, or for long. A clever chap would set the brake but always look for a stump or rock, or just the slight edge of the root swell of a tree, to butt a track against on the downhill side. Or set the brake but slide the front blade behind a stump or tree and apply hydraulic down pressure. To avoid scarring up the tree, we'd stop with the blade just an inch shy of touching the tree and set the brake. If the brake failed, the tree would stop the dozer. If the dozer was facing downhill, just burying the dozer blade into the ground would make her sit and stay. We learned these lessons throughout the course of our workday. The phrase "live and learn" was probably first whispered in prayer by a logger.

Art and I were working our way across a sidehill stand of timber. He'd bunched a beech perpendicular to the steep grade. Next, he went up the hill about thirty feet and off to the side to get a maple I'd cut down. I helped him hook on to it. We talked and agreed he would pull it out and bunch it above the beech, then get an ash, marked about twenty feet below the bunched beech that I'd yet to cut. I went to do so.

Art bunched the maple, hopped back on the dozer, and swung the rear of it downhill to get a straight cable pull toward the ash that I was cutting about forty feet away directly below him, past the bunched beech. He set the foot brake and climbed off the dozer. As he reached for a choker chain off the back, he heard the brake click off and he jumped out of the way. It almost ran over his feet.

The dozer took off flying down the hill. I was forty feet below it, my back to Art, ear plugs in, concentrating on cutting the ash. Art was running alongside the crawler, screaming, "Willy!" But he couldn't outrun the dozer as it came rolling down at me. On the hillside, about ten feet away from me, was the butt of the beech Art had bunched. His doing so saved me. When the left track of the dozer nicked the butt edge of the beech, it threw that side of the dozer up in the air about three feet. It turned it just enough to miss me. I sensed something and looked up from my cutting as the dozer flashed by me six inches away. It continued down the hill going hell-a-tee-ding-dong and smacked into a tree. Didn't hurt it a bit. I, on the other hand, had to sit down on a stump for a few minutes. I was shaking like a dog passing a pinecone.

Chapter 8
The Woods

There is something uniquely inspiring, daunting, challenging, and real about going into the woods to work for the day. All senses need to be fully engaged and in tune to the nourishing company of what is enduring and authentic about the forest. People who spend their days toiling within the confines of walls and roofs may seem to have all the advantages when compared to the logger. How do we quantify an advantage?

There is no scale to measure the benefit of seeing the sun peek over a ridge on a frost-covered morning. Or hearing the haunting call of a raven as it glides over the forest canopy above you. Blue jays and red squirrels squawking and chattering the latest gossip. Chickadees panhandling at lunch. The sights, sounds, and smells of the forest are a force that binds me to the land in a way that can't be reproduced. I know I'm not just visiting. I'm working with it; earning my living; living my life. The cycle of seed, tree, log, house, home, has been repeated for ages.

As I worked day after day in the woods I became part of a working landscape, shaping it in ways that mattered and had long-lasting consequences. I was performing a service to the forest in places that may not be serviced again for years. Art and I worked our tails off because we loved it. Running a chainsaw involved hard, physically demanding work. It meant tough mental challenges and decisions—ones that can alter the health and resilience of the forest for decades. And now I felt the need to do it in the best way I could.

Picking and preparing a spot, or *bed*, for a large tree to lie in takes time, knowledge, and patience. Having the skill to lay the tree into the bed takes expertise. Punching in skid roads with the bulldozer, to work with the landscape instead of against it, requires knowledge of the soils and terrain and a ton of talent with the dozer. Bunching trees in such a manner that the trees left standing aren't all scarred up requires finesse, cleverness, and ability. I didn't drive dozer much when I started out, but by watching Art, I knew how to do it, and how to do it right.

When I picked up a chainsaw every morning and walked toward the first tree of the day, I began a process that became second nature in one way, but a matter of life and death in another. Even a small tree can kill me. It'll kill me just as dead as a large one. If I ever became casual about the dangers that surrounded each tree I approached, I knew it was upping the odds against me. The ice I skated on would get thinner. And just like no ice is safe ice, even when I took all the precautions, there were still unseen dangers—perils that wouldn't come into play until things started to happen. I'm reminded of the board game Mouse Trap I played as a kid. An assemblage of a sequence of seemingly unrelated events ends up with a mouse being caught. But this was a game with much higher stakes.

Each tree to cut has to be evaluated to see if dangers are waiting around or above where the cutter needs to work. When the leaves are on the trees and the canopy is thick and lush, it can be quite difficult to see dead limbs. And when the trees are bare, it can be even harder, because they all look like they might be dead. It's hard to tell the dead limbs from the live ones. Rain and snow can be blowing in your face or sweat gets in your eyes as you squint up into a hot, humid, sun-drenched forest.

Maybe it's the last hitch of a long, hard day and you falter down the home stretch—lose sight of your goal to stay safe just when you need to have a bead on it—like a drunk who concentrates long enough to drive home from a night of drinking and totals the car in the driveway. Logging becomes a lethal balancing act, weighing the time it takes to be safe against the time it takes to be productive, to get the wood out, to pay the bills.

When a tree starts to fall in rough terrain, escape routes can be tricky. Scrambling away on a sidehill means unsure footing. While watching where you're going, things could be happening above you that need to be seen. I've never liked to run blindly down my escape path. Many times I've had limbs come pounding down out of the forest canopy and into my path. If I'd been running instead of watching, I would've run right under it. I learned to ease away from the tree as it started to fall. As my eyes constantly searched for danger from above, I'd feel my way with my feet while I moved away carefully, yet ready to move quickly.

Often I've had to react and leap one way or the other to dodge a limb. And when a limb comes from forty feet up, pointy-end first, it doesn't have to be that thick or long to hurt like hell. I've had them buckle my knees and shatter my hard hat—all by falling limbs that I never saw coming despite my best efforts.

Getting bruised and banged up became the norm I learned to accept. I'd see bruises when I showered and didn't know how they got there. Black and blue badges of combat that would blossom and fade, swell and recede. They never stopped me from working or sent me to the doctor's. Some sure made me wince and limp around for a few days.

Chapter 9
Bound Up and Pinched Tight

When Art and I were hammering out seventy or eighty trees a day, we would get into a rhythm and a pace with each other. As the cutter, when I would be running my chainsaw, my primary focus would be on doing that, as it should be. The tip of the chainsaw has to be considered as some sort of high-powered, poisonous snake that can turn and bite you without warning. If the tip unexpectedly encounters debris that hits the zipping, sharp chain's teeth at the right angle, that snake will strike. It's called a kickback, and it can throw the chainsaw bar upward or downward faster than a person can react and with more force than a man can stop. Chain brakes on chainsaws were designed precisely for this phenomenon that tends to lacerate the upper torso, neck, and head. But even a stopped chain can still lay open a flap of flesh and ruin a logger's rugged good looks.

The nature of a chainsaw's chain is that it takes a chunk out of the wood. Or flesh. It has two similar, yet opposing, sets of teeth on alternating side-straps of the chain, every other link.

The one on the right side cuts up and over to the left at a ninety-degree angle; the one on the left cuts up and over to the right. Think of them as the side, corner, and top of a razor-sharp, three-eighths-inch-wide, narrow rectangle. Whatever is inside the little rectangle is toast. Sawdust. Hamburg. This is what creates the width of the cut, called the kerf, which allows for the thickness of the chainsaw's bar to pass through the wood without binding.

Cutting the limbs off a tree is a tedious process that requires good footing, a solid stance, and a sharp focus on each limb being cut. What amount and direction of tension was applied to the limb as the tree fell? Even gravity applies a certain amount of tension on a tree limb as it hangs free in the air. Cut on the wrong side of the limb and it will bind the chain. Getting your chainsaw bound or pinched in a cut is a mistake that doesn't go away, but hopefully gets less frequent. It's a matter of odds that now and then, tension on a limb will be contrary to what was thought, especially when using the SWAG method (scientific wild-ass guess). Just when I'd got pretty good with keeping my saw from binding, and gone days and even weeks without doing so, a simple cut would clamp down on my saw like the jaws of life, all because the tension on the limb wasn't what I believed.

How does a person get the chainsaw unbound when it gets pinched in a cut, you ask? Well, there's the old "yank-and-twist" method—fun and satisfying if nothing else, mostly because the operator is pissed off. If it isn't pinched too deep, this has been known to work on occasion. On other, less happy occasions, it has bent the chain and broken the handle mounts on the chainsaw.

If it's stuck in a large cut, such as when a tree is topped off, there is the possibility of using one of the felling wedges the cutter possesses and pounding it into the kerf of the cut, freeing up the chainsaw. I kept a hatchet on the bulldozer for driving wedges and hacking and flailing at limbs that had my saw bound-up. Another stress-relieving activity that's a real money-maker.

Sometimes I would have Art use the crawler's winch to pull a little on the downed tree I was bound in to shift the weight of the tree. This was chancy because it might roll the wrong way and bust the chainsaw or bend the bar and chain. I'd stay next to my saw in the tree so I could muckle onto it as soon as it freed up. The most reliable method is to use a second chainsaw to cut out the stuck one. In my later years while working alone, I always kept a second chainsaw handy to facilitate freeing a pinched saw. Hot Tip: Don't get the second one bound up too.

One of the worst ways a logger can bind the saw is in the back cut of a tree being felled. To avoid this, I would tap an aluminum or plastic wedge in behind the chainsaw bar once the back cut was far enough along to allow it. It would keep the tree from rocking back onto the chainsaw's bar. There are some trees the dozer can't get close enough to, to push over. The only way to get them to fall in the direction needed is to wedge them over by hand—a procedure that keeps you warm on winter days and sweating like a musk ox during the heat of the summer.

Art and I were cutting and bunching in Eden. One breezy summer day found us on some brutal, rough ground. To say it was rough was like saying an alligator is a bit nippy. The area was strewn with boulders and rock and ledge that made getting around with the bulldozer very restrictive. I had a huge sugar maple marked to cut, up on a ledge, surrounded by a lot of boulders. The tree was leaning the wrong way to make for easy removal. Hell, if it went in the wrong place, it could get stuck between boulders and never come out. There was no way to get the dozer up to it to push it over in the right direction. It had to be wedged over.

There was a four-inch-diameter beech sapling in the bed where I was hoping to lay the maple. I cut it down and cut a three-foot club from it to use to pound my wedge. I cut my notch, or what some call a scarf, and started on my back cut. When I'd cut a bit over halfway, I pulled the aluminum felling wedge out of my hip pocket and drove it snug into the back cut on the opposite side of the scarf using my club. As I continued my back cut, I felt the tree trying to rock back in the fickle wind that was blowing. I stopped and drove on the wedge a few more whacks. Then I finished the cut, leaving what I figured to be adequate hinge holding.

I picked up my beechwood bat and commenced driving on the wedge. It wasn't going in for beans. Nertz! The wind wasn't helping any. I cut a bit more off my hinge and wailed some more on the wedge. Now the wind had started to rock it back and forth, and I'd made a little progress when it rocked the right way. I walked around to the scarf, took my saw and reached into it, cut a little, teeny-tiny bit, just in the center of the three-foot-diameter sugar maple. This left less hinge wood to wedge against, and I hoped it would make it easier to pound over. But now I had this monster maple, hanging by a hair of a hinge, on a boulder-strewn mountainside, with the wind kicking up a gale. Oh boy! This was getting more fun by the minute!

I kept pounding on the wedge and got it in most of the way, but now I was getting riled because the tree still wasn't falling. I picked up the saw again, reached into my back cut, and started nipping at the hinge very, very, carefully. Out of the wild blue yonder, a big gust of wind came roaring across the mountainside. The tree made a loud CRACK! as it broke the hinge wood, pinching my chainsaw in the back cut. Fudge! The tree hung there for a second, then began a slow, graceful turn on the stump and started to fall, but not in the desired direction. Time for a little dancing lesson with a monster maple!

I was down on one knee, waltzing around with the turn of the tree, pulling and praying, but the chainsaw wasn't budging. I knew that when this tree fell into all those rocks, there was a goddamn good chance the butt that I was kneeling next to would fly into the air, swing, and pivot around God-knew-where. I didn't want to be in the vicinity when it did. But, hell, I didn't want to leave my chainsaw to get crushed, neither!

All this happened in seconds, but it seemed like minutes. I was there with both hands on my chainsaw, my head craned upward at this giant tree, which was trying to kill me, in its death throes. A limb broke off up in the canopy, but I saw that was going to miss me. The tree rolled off one of its neighbors and kept twisting toward the ground, and I grabbed my chainsaw as it finally broke free. I turned and ran like I had someplace to go and it was on fire. The ground shook and the forest behind me exploded in a brief, brutal fury as the huge hardwood reluctantly came to rest.

Getting a chainsaw bound in a cut or pinched in a limb isn't a grave danger in and of itself. But what you're doing when it pinches, and the antics needed to get it loose can hijack you into a whole new world of terror. The time wasted trying to get a chainsaw unbound is time that trees aren't being cut and wages are lost. A smashed chainsaw is a couple weeks' wages shot to hell. Bent saw bars and saw chain, broken motor mounts and handlebars cost money—money that's earned by sweat and toil, muscle and skill. But if you run a chainsaw cutting trees, sooner or later, it's bound to happen.

Chapter 10
Dead Trees Standing

Courses in chainsaw safety and proper tree-felling protocol instruct the cutter to look for dead stubs in the working area and to cut them down before working nearby. But they often don't tell how to safely cut down dead stubs. The chore of dealing with dead stubs isn't a choice activity for a logger. There can be many on the woodlot. If a cutter was to drop them all, he'd have little time to cut paying timber. Too, there's the fact that dead stubs are more difficult and dangerous to cut than a live tree. They lack decent, strong hinge wood to control the direction of fall, so they can go anywhere. Frequently do. And when one does, if it hits another tree, it can break and sort of fold in half and come back at the cutter who has to tap-dance his way out of range.

Pushing them over with equipment is another option. Not a good one, mind you, but an option nonetheless. This procedure can often cause chunks of the stub to rain down on the equipment. They can put dents in equipment, and possibly the driver, and scare the hell out of him as an added bonus. Many stubs need to be notched with a chainsaw and back cut a bit to give them a direction to fall when pushed with equipment. This must be done very cautiously. And keep everybody a good tree-length or better away from any stub being pushed by equipment. Don't be standing around gawking.

One of the benefits of leaving a dead stub standing when safety allows is because of the number of creatures who rely on them for food and shelter. The insects that live inside of stubs are daily meals for birds. And the holes drilled out by woodpeckers become nesting cavities for a variety of critters. It bothered me when I cut down a stub and saw a family of squirrels or mice go scurrying away. Just seeing nesting material scattered about from the smashed-up remains, I'd feel remorse. I knew I'd ruined somebody's home. I'd caused them to be exposed to the elements and predators and might've got them killed. Just like I might've been killed if I hadn't taken the precaution of putting the stub on the ground.

Dad often told me that all a man can do is the best he can and let the rough end drag. The best I could do was drop the ones needed to stay safe and work around the others with an eyeball peeled. It was always a judgment call, and it could be wrong. Dead wrong.

I had felled a tree while Art was bunching others I had dropped, and I was eager to get the next hitch bunched for the skidder. The tree—a large, straight white ash—had barely stopped bouncing before I was working my way down the left side of it, snipping off the limbs scattered along its length. I would stop, get a solid stance, and cut off what limbs I could reach; move ahead to the next bunch of limbs on the tree, stop, get a solid stance, and cut off what limbs I could reach. Rinse, lather, and repeat. I took a couple steps ahead to the next limbs when the whole tree shook. I turned and looked behind me. A dead stub, thirty feet tall and about twenty feet away, had fallen out of the woods perpendicular to the tree I was working on. It hit four feet behind me. If it had fallen ten seconds earlier, I would've been standing there. It would've flattened me like an old felt hat. And they say cats have nine lives.

Chapter 11
Hell on Wheels

Art and I spent a hell of a lot of time together. We'd ride to work each day in my Datsun B-210. It was an hour's drive from where we were living in Essex up to Glenn's log job in Eden. One September morning we set out bright and squirrely to get there at seven for another day of cutting and bunching. We were on Route 100-C just outside of Johnson, and I was beating that car like I'd stole it.

The road went uphill through a series of turns before it topped out into a long straightaway. We were driving through the turns, yacking away about something. Suddenly, all conversation ceased. We were almost to a left-hand turn when we saw a huge boat of a Buick coming downhill through the turn, skidding sideways, doing sixty! There was no time for brakes and nowhere to go. There were guardrails on both sides of the road, and the Buick was taking up the whole freaking highway! For a brief second, I knew we were going to collide, and my only thought was "Brace yourself!"

With an earsplitting, crashing, smashing, crunching THUD! my car plowed into the passenger door and front tire of the Buick. Then Art and I were going backwards, shoved down the highway and pushed along the guardrails. The little Datsun finally spun free and came to a stop. In a deafening silence, Art and I sat there, stunned, almost in disbelief as to what in the hell just happened.

"Holy shit, Art! Are you okay!?"

"Yeah, Willy! Are you!?"

"I think so," I said, but I'm still dazed."

Smoke and steam were seeping out from under the crumpled hood of my car, and I was thinking it might burst into flames any second.

"Let's get the hell out of this thing before it blows!"

We unbuckled our seatbelts and shoulder harnesses, something we were able to do because we'd met Pete, Crazy from Chazy. The advice he'd given Art and me about buckling up had been put in practice—a habit acquired because I'd chosen the forest instead of college. A choice made when I'd realized I needed to follow my dreams, no matter what. A reality I learned because on a beautiful summer morning, my mom walked out to the garden and there was dew on the grass. She saved my life. Sometimes, when I thought things were falling apart, maybe things were just falling into place.

Art got out his side of the crumpled car, but I couldn't get my door open because it was smashed. The front tire was sticking through the floorboards, and the brake pedal was bent over the gas pedal. The steering wheel was bent some, where I braced myself when we hit. I gave up on trying to get my door open and started to climb over the center console, but was having trouble.

At first I couldn't believe my eyes. Halfway between my hip and my knee, my left leg was grotesquely twisted. Grabbing it, I saw, on the left side, the ragged edge of a shattered bone sticking out of my jeans. With the palm of my left hand, I shoved the bone back in. I didn't think about it. I had to do it. I couldn't stand seeing that bone sticking out! I guess I thought that maybe if I shoved it back in, everything would be okay. Thankfully, because of the adrenalin rushing through my veins, I didn't feel a damn thing.

"Art! My leg's busted! Get me the hell out of here!"

He came back to see me stranded between the seats and took a gander at my leg.

"Oh shit, Willy! Grab on!" Art latched onto me as I grabbed onto him, and he lifted me out of the car, carried me to safety, and laid me on the ground by the guardrails, his wadded-up jacket under my head. In less than five minutes, we heard the sirens coming. The ambulance crew had just gotten back from a call when the one for me came in. They hopped back in the ambulance and were at the site in a few minutes. I guess you could call it a lucky break. Art didn't get a scratch, and the girl driving the Buick? She didn't bust a pimple.

The femur is the largest bone in the body, and mine was snapped clean off in the middle of it. It was the straightest break of a femur the surgeon had ever seen. He told me this as he explained my two options. One was to remove the marrow from the bone and pound a 17-inch stainless steel rod inside of it from the end located at the top of my ass. The rod would hold the two busted pieces of bone together while it healed. I could be out of the hospital on crutches in two weeks. The other was I could spend twelve weeks flat on my back with my leg in traction. I told him the rod pounding deal sounded like more fun than spitting off a bridge. They prepped me for surgery.

During the operation I was heavily sedated, but as I lay on the operating table, I can still remember the doctor telling the interns, as he started to pound on the rod, "Hold him still. I don't want to miss." The clear ringing sound of steel hitting steel and my whole body shaking with each blow is something that will stick with me forever.

I left the hospital ten days later on a pair of crutches and was taken in by my favorite aunt and uncle to convalesce. I'll be forever grateful for their generosity. I was in no shape to take care of myself. I didn't have a vehicle or means of making money. There'd be a lot of work ahead to get my leg back in shape before I could return to the woods.

The accident happened in September, and by January, I thought I was ready to try logging again. I found work cutting for a guy in Waterbury. He was doing a job at Little River State Park. The snow was deep that year, and the going was brutal in the woods. I lasted about three weeks before my leg got too painful to continue. An x-ray showed that the rod in my leg had moved outward. The doctor said it had "migrated," like it was a caribou heading across the tundra. He also said my busted leg was a half inch shorter than my right one. I figured it'd be handy for working sidehills.

Chapter 12
Back at It

Spring came that year and along with it my hopes of getting a job doing what I knew would be my life's work. The woods meant more to me than just a place to earn a living. It was where I belonged, where I had a sense of place as well as purpose. I'd laid down a lot of timber since I'd picked up my first chainsaw. I was no longer a greenhorn, though still far from an expert. I had cut thousands of trees and had become more knowledgeable in just about every aspect of the logging trade. And I enjoyed the physical, day-long hours of labor that's needed to get the timber roadside. It was no surprise to me that I found another job without too much searching.

Peen Whiffle gave Art and me a job cutting and skidding for him on a lot he had in Duxbury. He was looking for a crew to run his equipment while he worked at IBM. He'd bought a spanking-new John Deere 440C Skidder and a nice little John Deere 350C bulldozer. He didn't know diddley about logging, but apparently he had enough money to burn a wet mule. He also had one of the steepest skid roads Art and I had ever seen. It was so steep that going down it without a hitch of logs wasn't advised, as the skidder might go end-over-end without the weight of the hitch behind it. And going up it empty was no picnic either. There were a few spots where, for thirty feet or so, it was bare ledge nearly straight up.

The JD 440C has a little pedal behind your right foot called a differential lock. It allows the operator to lock all four wheels to turn together without one or more wheels slipping and spinning. With chains on all four tires and the differential locked in, it could creep up these steep sections. It had to be in first gear and the engine at an idle. It might slip and slide back a foot or two now and again and take your breath away and give your stomach butterflies, but it would scratch its way up eventually.

One morning the John Deere salesman, Marcel LaPlant, showed up to see how things were going with the new machines. We were just getting ready to head up the mountain.

"How you boys like the new skidder, eh? She doing all right?" he asked as I got my chainsaw, gas, and bar oil jugs onto the skidder.

"I've done a bit of logging me-self. I loved driving de skidder. I wish I'd never left de woods." He was all puffed up like a little bantam rooster.

Art and I looked at each other and smiled. We'd talked to Marcel before. One of the greatest bullshitters you'd ever meet. He lied so much he probably had to get somebody else to call his dog, which was probably what made him such a good salesman. The guy could sell a bull moose a hat rack.

"Oh yeah?" Art said," Why don't you hop on the front of her and come see for yourself? We're just heading up to get a hitch."

"I'd love to, eh, but I can't stay too long."

"We have a hitch all cut and bunched. It won't take long at all."

Art and I made a practice of having a hitch all set to go for the morning when we quit at the end of the day. It just felt good to know that you had a jump on things right off the bat. Plus, the skidder driver could head out and get to work.

"Hell, I'll even let you take the hitch out. It'll be just like old times."

"Oh, why not?" Marcel said. "It is a nice day to be out in de woods, eh?"

He got onto the skidder blade, Art lifted it up, and Marcel sat there on the hood, holding onto the limb risers. I scrunched into the edge of the cab beside Art, who was grinning like a butcher's dog as we headed up the goat path that served as our skid road.

We snaked our way up the mountain, with Marcel perched out front like a French Canadian hood ornament. When we approached the first steep spot, he turned and looked at us with his eyes bugged out and Art yelled, "Hang on!" but I don't think it was necessary. We made it up by the skin of our teeth and came to a stop next to our bunched hitch of trees. Marcel jumped off before Art could lower the blade for him. He was a bit pale.

"Y-yous guys are t-touched in de head!" he stammered as he began trotting back down the road.

"Wait a minute!" Art yelled after him. "Don't you want to take her down?"

Marcel turned and looked at us like we were nuttier than a squirrel turd.

"Not me no. I wouldn't drive it down dat road for a thousand dollars!" he shouted back.

"Hell," answered Art, "I do it four or five times a day for a lot less!"

Art and I looked at each other and started laughing as Marcel jogged out of sight.

"I thought he loved driving skidder."

"Christ almighty, Art, he's so full of shit his eyes are brown."

Marcel never dropped by again. We finished that job with everything still in one piece, including Art and me.

Chapter 13
Trouble Comes in Threes

Peen moved us to another woodlot he'd contracted to cut on Milo White Road in Jericho. Events that occurred while working there stand out like a three-legged racehorse. The first happened because of a simple, brief lapse of memory, otherwise known as a brain fart.

I had a sixteen-inch DBH hemlock to cut that was positioned about four feet down a slope leading to a stream. I cleared away some old branches on the ground around the tree and noticed there was a very old, twelve-inch-diameter, knee-high stump about three feet away from the hemlock. It left me just enough room to work at cutting down the tree. As I finished the last cut in my felling notch and was drawing my chainsaw down and through the cut toward me, I took a step backward. Oops. I had forgotten about the old stump behind me. It tripped me in such a manner that I sat down on top of it. I couldn't keep my chainsaw from sitting down in my lap too. It landed with the motor on my right thigh, the chainsaw bar across my left thigh, the chain still churning at a good clip.

Chainsaw safety chaps are filled with Kevlar, the same material used in bullet-proof vest. The strength-to-weight ratio is five times that of steel. I had on a pair. The material is such that it binds up in the chain and clutch sprocket of the chainsaw and stops the chain. Before it did, the chain went through the chaps and through my jeans. One tooth on the chain laid over a two-inch flap of flesh on my left thigh about a quarter inch deep. Yikes! Ruining a fifty-dollar pair of chaps was a hell of a lot cheaper than a visit to the ER I have no doubt I would've cut my leg right to the bone if not for those chaps. If it had cut the femoral artery I'd have bled out sitting on that old stump. But damn it, they was one of my favorite pairs of jeans!

This was the first time I'd ever cut myself, and it scared the hell out of me. But the burned hand teaches best, or in this case, the cut leg. I would never again feel the bite of a chainsaw for the rest of my career. As for the slice on my leg, I took a couple of Band-Aids, taped the wound shut, and worked my way out of it.

The little John Deere 350C bulldozer we were using could go just about anywhere, As Art would prove quite often. Getting as close as possible to felled trees can save pulling winch cable, and thus time and energy. The fact that sometimes the best trees were in the hardest places to get at would lead us into some nasty spots. These trees were overlooked by previous loggers because they were hard to get, and years before, they were smaller too. Now that they'd matured, with market prices higher, they were worth going after. Art and I would sometimes use all hundred feet of cable on the crawler's winch and have to tie two or three of his eight-foot-long chokers together to reach some of the trees. Some days we'd work until dark and be back at it come daylight.

One day we were working our way along the side of a ridge, steeper than hell and rougher than a boar's ass with rock and ledge. Then we got into the bad part. Art backed the dozer down a steep, short grade, jockeying around trees and over rocks to get close to a group of marked trees down the ridge near the boundary line. He was truly between a rock and a hard place, barely room to maneuver. As he braked one track and backed up, a straight-edged chunk of ledge under the bulldozer lined up perfect as the track slid against it and peeled the track off the front idler sprocket to the outside, away from the engine. He was looking behind him to see where he was going and didn't realize there was a problem until it had also come off the rear drive sprocket! It was hogged up and wedged in against the final-drive housing. Well, don't that take the rag off the bush!

If you've ever heard of the expression "going at something hammer-and-tongs," this would be an accurate description of the work performed by Art and me. We went at it hammer-and-tongs and pry-bars-and-come-alongs and tire-jacks-and-anything-else-we-could-lay-our-hands-on. It took a day and a half of jacking and prying and cussing and pounding to get that sucker back on the sprockets, mostly because of the inaccessibility of where it was positioned on the side of a rock and boulder-strewn ridge.

This was ten times worse than any track work we'd ever done. I got a thorough schooling on the vulgarity of bulldozer track assemblage and repair. I had skinned knuckles and blood blisters in places I never thought possible. I began to wonder if I'd ever make enough money logging to pay for a hernia operation.

It was the last Saturday of July when Art and I went in to work. This day had a special significance. Art was getting married, and he was nervous as a grasshopper in a chicken coop. We weren't supposed to be working, but he said the only thing to calm him down was to cut a hitch or two. As his best man, I felt obligated to support his choice on how to spend his remaining hours as a bachelor.

We were going to work just half a day as his wedding was at two o'clock. Around ten, I was coming onto the landing with a hitch behind me on the skidder. I drove the front left wheel of her onto the decked logs about six feet from the end of the pile. I planned to drive up and over the pile and drop my hitch right on the end of it to simplify cutting the stems into logs. I'd done it previously, but the pile was a bit higher now. I drove up on it, with the left front wheel going over the logs and the right wheel starting to. The left rear tire began to climb onto them as well. I was at a pretty good tilt, with the weight of the hitch wanting to tip me over as I readied to release the winch to drop the load. My timing was a bit off.

The left front wheel of the skidder was pawing on the topmost log, and when I dropped the hitch, I just hung there for a second or two. Then the skidder rolled to the right, down off the logs, and laid on its side like a beached whale. It all happened in slow motion. I just held on like grim death and didn't get a scratch. I had the presence of mind to kill the engine as soon as I pried my fingers lose.

Art was to walk out as soon as he had finished bunching a couple trees. Walking up the skid road, I met him half-way. I told him what happened and persuaded him to head on home and get ready for the wedding while I got the bulldozer and drove it to the landing to flip the skidder upright.

Peen happened to stop by with a friend to show off his equipment on the log job. When they pulled onto the landing and saw his skidder lying there on its side, he got all steamed up. I told him to bank his fire and that everything would be fine and dandy. It wasn't long before I had the skidder back on all fours. I let it sit for fifteen minutes so the engine oil could seep back to where it needed to be, and it fired right up. It bellowed black smoke for a while, but then cleared up just fine. Sort of like Peen. I made it to Art's wedding just in time to see them joined in wedded bliss.

Working for somebody else wasn't all that lucrative. Getting paid by the tree, or by the amount of timber cut, meant there was a lot of pressure to produce a large volume. I still had to supply my own chainsaw, gas, and bar oil and work as a subcontractor without insurance. Nobody made a nickel unless I fired up my saw and started cutting down trees. If I was going to keep risking my neck every day, I wanted the rewards from doing so and felt ready for the responsibility.

Growing up is never straightforward, but I was taking some steps. I'd found the love of my life. Karen was prettier than a Christmas package, and after two years of courting and sparking her, I persuaded her to marry me. Now it was time to pursue the love of the woods that I had been chasing since I was a pup—and to do it on my terms, in the way I felt the forest deserved. I had to hire a lawyer, but I finally got settled up with the insurance company of the girl that crashed her car into me. I used the money to start my own logging business.

Art decided to pursue other options. As we mature, we find out who we are and what we want from life. Sometimes, people that we love and respect follow different paths and that's okay. We would remain the best of friends for the rest of our lives. There would always be a bond between us. A trust that never weakened. Art would always be my sounding board when I was confounded by the hardships logging brought to my doorstep. He was my woods-wise therapist, his credentials measured in the miles of winch cable he had pulled, roads punched in, logs on the landing—earned in the woods being whipped by the winter winds and seared by the summer heat. Art and I had a connection that cutting and bunching together had pulled snug as a choker on a tree. Like two guys sharing a foxhole, we'd been in the war together, served side-by-side in the elite outfit of all those slaying trees in the North Woods.

Chapter 14
The Lone Logger

I elected not to buy a skidder as my means to get wood roadside. Even the smallest skidders weren't that small or maneuverable and required a fairly wide path to get to the trees. And all you can do with a skidder is skid wood. I decided I would purchase a four-wheel-drive farm tractor and equip it for the woods. Companies were starting to develop reliable, three-point-hitch, power takeoff (PTO)–driven winches for tractors that enabled them to function as a capable way to skid trees out of the woods.

I made the choice to go as small as possible but still have the ability to skid a large tree if cut into logs. I would keep my skidding distances short by working on smaller woodlots. I also wanted to be able to cut, split, and deliver firewood to folks' homes. I would return to how I started when I cut wood for my dad on shares. This would allow the removal of low-grade hardwood from clients' woodlots, a necessary procedure to improve the quality of the timber stand.

Hardwood pulp wasn't worth much, and I had to get twelve cord on the landing for a truckload. This requires a lot of room on the landing, as do the tractor trailer and loader needed to ship it. Landing space is often limited on small woodlots. However, split and delivered hardwood firewood paid a much higher price per cord. It did mean more time and labor, which made small woodlots take longer to harvest.

I knew I wouldn't be able to move large volumes because I was only one man. I decided my plan would be to skid the least amount of wood for the most amount of money. I would promote the quality of my work, the light-on-the-land impact of my equipment, and the ability to do small jobs that other, larger operators weren't interested in.

I bought a used Chevy C-30 one-ton truck with a dump box. It would hold a cord of split firewood without having to stack the wood in the box. I searched around for a good four-wheel-drive tractor, and purchased a new SAME 60 horsepower, air-cooled diesel with a bucket loader. The SAME brand is a subsidiary of Lamborghini, which makes wicked good race cars, so I figured their tractors would skid the wood out faster than a buttered bullet. I took the tractor to my dad's garage and we put a belly pan under it and limb risers and a steel canopy on top. Dad also made a small decking blade for pushing up logs, because the wide bucket on the loader restricted maneuverability through the woods.

I bought a Farmi three-point-hitch winch for the tractor that would pull about eight thousand pounds. I thought it would be plenty, since the tractor only weighed about five thousand. I found out it was nothing like a bulldozer or skidder winch that pulls about twenty thousand pounds. I learned I had to set my chokers and hook the cable onto the logs with more thought and precision to roll them around rocks and roots that other winches would've pulled right through.

Now that I had equipment, I needed a woodlot to work on. The Ethan Allen Firing Range consists of eleven thousand acres of mostly forested property located near my home in West Bolton. Josh Besse was the forester who managed the land available outside of the various danger zones and *cone of fire* where General Electric tested its guns.

Josh had marked a small timber sale on the range that he put out for bid. I was one of three guys who attended the bid showing. The trees marked were mostly firewood with a few saw log–size trees scattered about. Pretty scurvy stuff. I put in a bid, and much to my surprise, I won the job. Or lost, depending on how you looked at it. It wasn't until after I'd signed the contract that Josh told me I was the only bidder.

My dog Wolfie, a German wirehaired pointer I'd had for six years, kept me company as I worked my tail off on that shot-up job all winter. I would hit bullets buried in the trees while I was cutting them into firewood—steel, armor-piercing bullets that would tear the teeth off my chainsaw's chain. I didn't dare to send any logs to a sawmill. The chance of ruining their expensive saw blades and having them come after me for the cost was too great. If they sawed into bullets, it wouldn't take a genius to figure out they came from the guy working on a firing range.

Chapter 15
A Hairy Story

In mid-December I got an order to deliver a cord of firewood to an address on Route 15 in Underhill. I threw a cord on my truck, and with Wolfie riding shotgun, headed out to deliver it. When I arrived at the address and pulled into the driveway, I was met by a couple standing next to a rusty old pickup truck. I'll call the guy "Hairy" because things got that way. Also to avoid nuisance litigation.

Hairy was about six-foot three with long, greasy, brown hair, beard, and teeth. His girlfriend—well, let's just say they were a matched set. You could've used her to cure hiccups. Hairy pointed up his long, twisting, uphill driveway that had about a foot of snow on it. I saw where other vehicles had got stuck and had to back down. Hairy told me to drive up it and dump the wood by the house at the top of the driveway.

I looked at him and I said, "Mister, there's no way I'm going to make it up that driveway with all the snow on it."

Well Hairy didn't want to hear that. He told me, quite rudely, that I should give it a try. I figured, what the hell, I'll humor the guy. I put the truck in gear and headed up the driveway. I went maybe a third of the way up and the truck started jigging and spinning. I stopped and carefully started backing down, trying to stay out of the ditch.

Hairy, who had followed me up the hill, is now following me back down the hill, standing in front of my truck and screaming and swearing at me like a crazy man, which I was starting to think is an accurate description of the jerk. As I got down to where his truck was parked, I saw there was room for me to turn around and I backed in. I had my window rolled down so I could see my side-view mirror better, and Hairy came up to it mad as hops, screaming and swearing. He told me I was a worthless, shitty driver and my truck is a piece of shit and to dump the wood right there.

Well that wasn't going to happen. There was no way in living hell I was going to dump my load of wood after the way this guy had treated me. I didn't trust the idiot to pay me, either. I looked at Hairy and I said, "Mister, you can go piss up a rope. Get your wood someplace else."

In hindsight, this probably wasn't the best choice of words, because Hairy reached into the truck window to grab me. Remember Wolfie riding shotgun? Wolfie and I were tight. He was about eighty pounds of muscle and bone, and he came across my lap with a growling lunge and caught a chunk of Hairy's coat sleeve as he yanked his arm out of the truck and went ass-over-tea-kettle into the snowbank behind him.

I took this as a signal to vacate the premises. I shoved Wolfie back to the passenger side, threw my truck in gear, and lit out down Route 15 like a big-ass bird. This left Hairy and his girlfriend standing in the middle of the road screaming obscenities and making crude hand gestures.

I breathed a deep sigh of relief, then sucked in a big gulp as I looked in my rearview mirror and saw Hairy's old truck come fleecing out of the driveway. She was behind the wheel, with Hairy hanging out the passenger side window, still screaming and yelling and flipping me off. I couldn't believe it. Even a toilet seat can only handle one asshole at a time. Now I had two chasing me down the highway!

They blew by me and then slowed down, trying to get me to stop. When we got almost stopped and there was no traffic coming, I pulled out and went around, and they came after me again. This time I didn't let them get by me, and as I came into Essex, I saw an Essex Police cruiser parked at a convenience store and I pulled in alongside of it.

The cruiser was unoccupied, so I bailed out of my truck and ran for the store like a Kentucky show horse. As I approached the door, I saw the reflection in the glass of Hairy's truck pulling in and he jumped out and was coming on the run. I stepped into the store and saw the police officer at the counter. It was Zane Snelling. He was about sixty years old and lived just a half mile down the road from where I grew up. We'd met. I ran up to him and I said, "Officer Snelling, we've got trouble and it's coming right behind me."

It did. Hairy came tearing into the store and ran up to me just a-cussing and swearing and said how he's going to drag my ass outside and beat the shit out of me. Ol' Zane stood there and stared at him with his mouth open, donut in one hand, coffee in the other. Finally he spoke up and said, "Now you watch your language."

I was thinking, "Really Zane? That's the best you got? Where's a hot-shot rookie when I need one?"

Hairy turned to Zane and told him to shut the hell up or else he's going to drag his ass outside and beat the shit out of him too. Zane stood there sucking wind.

Hairy turned back to me and said, "I'm going to get you, you son of a bitch! I'm going to find out where you live and I'm going make you pay! You and that goddamn dog of yours too!"

I consider myself a fairly easy-going individual. My dad taught me that life's a lot easier when you plow around the stumps. But you don't threaten a person's dog.

I stepped right up to that big, hairy moron and said, "I already know where you live, you stupid bastard!"

Well, I thought Hairy and I were going to start swinging right then and there. Evidently, he thought better of it, because he looked me in the eye for a couple seconds, said, "Fuck you!" and slammed his way out the door, hopped in his truck and peeled out down the road.

I turned to Zane and said, "Well officer, that didn't pan out the way I hoped."

I walked out to my truck and gave Wolfie a great big hug, thanked him for pulling my fat out of the fire, and drove on home. When I got there, Karen told me a guy named Hairy had called. Said he wanted to stop by and pay me if he knew where I lived. And she told him.

For the next month or so, I was packing heat everywhere I went. I was having nightmares of coming out of a store and finding Hairy standing by my truck to greet me. Karen kept telling me that I was overreacting. She says Hairy wasn't going to hurt anybody. And it turned out she was right. I opened the newspaper one morning, and there was a picture of Hairy. He's been arrested for robbing a bank. With a BB gun. I decided my chances of being attacked had diminished, so I put my real gun away.

When I added it all up, I'd cut and delivered sixty-five cords of firewood from that bullet-riddled piece of woods on the Firing Range. I learned about running my own business too. I worked the bugs out of my equipment and learned what it could and couldn't do. I also discovered that bidding on jobs could be a risky proposition. Trees could be hiding defects, and in this case bullets, that can't be readily seen. I also learned my people skills were fine. It was my tolerance of assholes that needed a little work.

Bill Hall was still the Chittenden County forester and had been forever. Years before, he had bestowed on Art and me a white-pine-weevilled woodlot of pecker-poles that we had lost our logging virginity on. Along with our shirts. I was hoping he might have a decent woodlot he'd let me cut and give me a chance to prove myself without having to go broke.

Bill had a new assistant and figured that, since we were both starting out in our careers, he would pair us up. David Brynn was a lanky, curly-haired fellow with a degree in forestry from the University of Vermont, but I never held it against him. A few years after we started working together, my four-year-old daughter and I were riding in my truck to meet with him and cruise a woodlot. I told her we were going to meet the forester. She had a question for me.

"Daddy, will he be wearing a bear suit?"

"Well, honey, with David, you never know." I stand by my answer.

We had a working relationship that would span over thirty years, and a friendship that I've yet to see the end of.

Chapter 16
Holy Moses!

David showed me a woodlot in Hinesburg belonging to a nice couple named Earl and Barry. Of the one hundred acres they had, only about half of it was worth working on. The remainder was old fields that were being reclaimed by the forest. It wasn't exactly a lucrative woodlot.

In fact, I doubt that any other logger would have touched it. I was going to have to prove to David, Bill Hall, Earl and Barry, and myself, that a person could make a go of it by cutting precommercial stands of low-quality wood. And do it using small equipment that didn't tear up the woods and the log roads. I was determined to treat the land as if it were my own.

Because when it comes right down to the short and curly, it is our land, our community, our town, our Vermont. Good stewardship and respect for the land isn't just assigned to those who have their names on a deed. I believe it's the duty of all who work the land, toil within the watersheds, breath the clean air, drink the clean water, and depend on the many treasures healthy forests provide.

There were some decent things about the woodlot. It had good southwest exposure and an excellent road network. Five years previous, Art Yandow had been hired to construct roads with ditches and water bars that kept the water off the roadbed during heavy rains and spring run-offs. My plan was to use these roads with my Chevy C-30 firewood truck and have wood-bunching areas alongside the road where I would cut, split, and load the firewood onto the truck. This would avoid skidding on it and causing damage.

The water bars would have to be crossed, but still be effective, during the job. Most had roadside ditches that brought the water down to the water bar and across the road. I laid down fifteen-foot lengths of four-inch-diameter drainage pipe and covered them with gravel I hauled in. David was skeptical that these would work, thinking they would be too small and get plugged or flattened by the weight of my truck. To prevent this, I laid a four-inch-diameter pole along each side of the pipes and put a good foot or better of gravel over them and checked them regularly to keep them free of debris. They worked slick.

I was there all summer, and it was there I did my first brush-hogging with my tractor. There was one other reason I'd chosen a tractor instead of a skidder: I'd bought a new Woods brush hog, and Earl and Barry hired me to mow their fields and alongside the wood's roads. Mine was five feet wide. It's powered by the tractor's power takeoff shaft to spin two independent blades at 540 RPM It has a shear pin on the drive shaft, and I was glad it did. It could mow just about anything the tractor could run over, from trees to cement blocks, and debris can and does go in all directions at 540 RPM

The best thing about Earl and Barry's was the spectacular view from the hill the woods road meandered up. The Champlain Valley lay out before me, with the Adirondacks marching north and south on the other side of Lake Champlain. One hot, muggy, typical August afternoon, I was splitting up a load of firewood. I could see thunderheads building across the lake from the perch I had near the top of Lincoln Hill. I was almost loaded and was hoping to beat the storm and was splitting and throwing in wood to beat the band. I kept glancing now and again at the streaks of lightning and heard the rolling roar of thunder as the storm moved closer.

I've always loved a good thunderstorm. They've held my fascination since childhood. It got darker as the storm blotted out the sun to the southwest and a few big raindrops splattered around me. There came a cool gust of wind and I stood up tall and straight and embraced it with my arms uplifted like Charlton Heston parting the Red Sea in *The Ten Commandments*. I was sweating like a hairy ox, and it felt refreshing as all get-out. As I took a deep breath of the cool air, I caught the sweet, pungent odor of ozone as the gust front of the storm slammed into the hillside. Called down from the heavens, a bolt of lightning struck the woods fifty yards before me with such force and fury that it knocked me over backwards. It shattered a huge old poplar to pieces and left my ears ringing. I gathered myself up and staggered to the safety of my truck as the rain came down in gray sheets.

Thirty minutes later, the sun was out and shining, the gurgling of water running in the ditches, chuckling at my arrogance for forgetting my paltry place on God's green earth. I still love a good thunderstorm. But now I find a sheltered place where I can savor the show.

I cut, split, and delivered eighty-four cords of wood and sold thirty-two hundred board feet of spruce logs to a local mill. As a side note, I put up six thousand bales of hay from my in-laws' farm while I was resting. If I never touch another bale of hay in my life it'll be too soon. Midway through the summer, David Brynn showed me another woodlot near my home in West Bolton on the Notch Road. I signed the contract in September and had the comfort of knowing where I would be for the fall and winter.

But it was while cruising this new woodlot that I lost my boy-dog. During the hike, Wolfie tore into a porcupine. His snout and inside of his mouth were loaded with quills. I got him in my truck and took him to the vet's, breaking land-speed records because of the pain and terror he was in. The vet put him under anesthesia to remove the quills. I was in the waiting room when the vet came out and asked me to join him in the examination room.

Wolfie was still unconscious and had all the quills out. The vet said after he got done with the quills, he gave Wolfie an abdominal exam and had found a large tumor in his intestines. He had me feel for myself, and he wasn't fibbing. It felt like a tennis ball–sized lump. Besides the fact that I couldn't afford the operation, the vet said the rehab, if he survived, would be a painful, grueling slog. He said the best thing for Wolfie would be to end his suffering right now. I was in tears as I called my dad. He said he'd pay the bill, if that was what I wanted, but said I had to decide. I got Art on the phone. He always knew the right things to say when I was in a quandary. We talked it out.

Wolfie had given me loyalty and love every day. He saved my ass when Hairy tried to thump the snot out of me. Saved me from a beating. A true friend would return the favor. I held him in my arms as the vet put Wolfie down. I felt lower than a snake full of buckshot. But even when dealing with his death I still had to keep making a living. I'd use the sanctuary of the woods to heal my hurt.

Chapter 17
Bolton Notch Ass-Backwards

The forester decides what trees are to be cut by squirting paint on them. It's the logger who removes them that makes the forester's decision look like the right one. If the forester is the person painting the picture, the logger is his brush. It can look heavy-handed and sloppy, or it can look precise and logical. It rarely looks clean and tidy. Woods are healthier when there's a decent amount of woody debris on the forest floor. Limbs and tops from trees removed are the fertilizer for the remaining ones. But the human eye likes to see neatness and familiarity as it scans a woodlot. Nature takes a different view and will constantly weed its own garden with natural disturbances. Diversity is more than a catch-phrase in the woods and is just as important to strive for as it is within our social circles.

One of the ways I could have my work look esthetically pleasing to landowners was to utilize more of the tree I was cutting down. I would use as much wood as practical, down to four inches in diameter. This would still leave plenty of material in the woods. The remaining tops would be lopped down with my chainsaw to get the limbs closer to the ground. In fact, a clause in the contract said I couldn't leave any limbs sticking up higher than four feet. And I never liked that clause. I was sure a person who looked hard enough could find a violation somewhere, and that didn't set well with me.

Wading out into felled tops of trees slashing with a chainsaw is one of the most dangerous and unnecessary procedures a logger can perform. And for years, I agreed to do it. It was mostly done for appearances. Limbs might decompose a bit faster if they are in close contact with the ground, but it isn't worth the time, fossil fuel, or risk. Leaving the debris standing will often discourage deer from browsing on the seedlings that will sprout from the added sunlight hitting the forest floor. Deer don't like wading through brush any more than I do, and they don't have to lug a chainsaw.

The contract lopping clause didn't consider that while trying to lessen the damage to remaining trees, many times I would use the same opening in the forest canopy for multiple trees. Sometimes I'd have tops piled up that would exceed the required four-foot height no matter how much they were lopped. These piles of brush may look a bit unsightly to some, but they looked like home to rabbits, squirrels, mice and others seeking refuge from weather and predators. I had to rely on the forester and trust he would educate and convince the land owner that this lopping clause had to be tempered with common sense. Thankfully, the foresters I worked with were of top quality and I was never accused of a violation.

I hired Dicky Streeter to help me for the winter. Dicky lived just down the road from me and we'd known each other since we were kids. My dad had a deer camp a half mile down a dead-end road across from the Streeter house going back to the 1950s. Dicky had run a chainsaw since he was big enough to hang onto one and was just as competent as I was with it. Maybe more so.

I knew I'd want some help on this job, because I was going to be in Bolton Notch. I figured the snow would be deep enough for me to need a snorkel. I wasn't far off. Thankfully, my dad had made me a nice little shanty to keep on my landings. Ol' Glenn had always kept a shanty on his landings and I'd learned they were handier than a handle on a piss pot.

Having a shanty helps keep a fella working. Especially during the winter months. It's sort of a logging headquarters for the crew. Mine, like Glenn's, had a nice little woodstove in it. I could toast up a sandwich, heat up a bowl of soup. It was a warm, dry place to sharpen and work on my chainsaw. I would swap out gloves and mittens for dry ones between hitches. I even kept extra coats, pants, and socks handy. I had a radio to listen to and catch the weather report. On the days when it was colder than a polar bear's toenails and the wind was howling down the hills, the shanty would keep my hopes up.

My winter in the Notch set the bar for all winters in the woods to come. We had days when the temperature never got out of the single digits with wind chills below zero for days on end. Starting the tractor meant having to get there before sunup and put a small propane heater under the oil pan and drape a tarp over the tractor. Then I'd sit and keep an eyeball peeled on it from the shanty window to see if it was going to catch fire. After a half hour or so of that, I'd hook jumper cables from my truck to the battery of the tractor. If I didn't, the tractor's glow plugs that preheated the intake air would drain the battery and it wouldn't have enough charge left to turn the engine over.

The snow just kept coming. Every day. Down in Jericho, seven miles away, it would snow six inches. In the Notch it would snow a foot. We had to shovel around trees so there wouldn't be a four-foot-high stump come spring. We'd try to keep wood piled on the landing so that on the worst days, when it was too raw and dangerously windy to cut in the woods, we could at least work on the landing, blocking and splitting wood. The warm confines of the shanty would give us a welcome respite from the elements.

By mid-winter, we were in a deep freeze, with the snow nearing waist high. The wolves were eating the sheep just for the wool. On a brittle, cold day, Dicky and I blocked up a couple cord of firewood and were going to start splitting it up. It was when we went to start the wood splitter that we realized we were out of gas for it. We hopped in my Chevy one-ton to go down to Bolton Store on Route 2. We needed splitter gas and Dicky could use a cup of coffee.

There was a half-inch dusting of snow on the road as we eased down over the crest of Notch Road. Bolton Notch Road is the steepest road in the town. Maybe in Chittenden County. Even steeper than Bolton Valley Access Road, and that's saying something. As I crept the truck over the first pitch, it lost traction on the dusting of cold snow and we shot down that hill faster than a fat kid on a teeter-totter.

It's an awful, helpless feeling to be at the wheel of a vehicle and not have much control over it. I knew if I touched the brakes it would only make things worse. I'd lose the little control

I had, so I just tried to keep it pointed downhill between the six-foot snowbanks on each side. The profanity in the cab rose considerably as we slid sideways to the left. I steered into it and she came back around and then went sideways to the right. The cussing became more descriptive and pronounced. By then, we were probably going forty miles an hour and it felt like ninety. We straightened back out for a couple of seconds and then did a complete one-eighty, just as pretty as you please. Now we were going down the road backwards! I was pretending to be steering by using my side mirror, but lord knows if it was amounting to much.

It was the massive snowbanks that saved us. The truck edged off the left side of the road, nice and gradual. We plowed into the snowbank until we were almost completely buried out of sight. It took about a hundred yards for us to finally come to a halt. We stopped about five feet short of center-punching a huge beech tree! We climbed out and looked at the path we'd cut through the snow. There was a huge rock that we'd scraped the snow off of as we blasted by it. And by shit luck, like when a monkey writes a book, it was the only stretch without roadside trees on the whole hill.

We walked back up to the landing, got the tractor, and yanked the truck out of the snowbank and up the hill to where we began our little sleigh ride. We siphoned some gas out of the truck for the splitter, and Dicky decided he could make do without a cup of coffee. I thought seriously about keeping a clean pair of underwear in the shanty in case of similar events.

The Notch job ended in the spring. Dicky went off to seek other means of employment, though we would work together a few more times in the years ahead. The landowner was tickled pink with my work, as well as David Brynn and Bill Hall. I would come back to that land in future years: once to clear an access road for Art Yandow to construct, another to cut a bit more firewood. The woodlot was coming along, and I hoped to come back some day and cut some saw log–size timber. I never did. The landowner listened to a smooth-talking logger cutting on adjacent property who enticed him with the promise of big money and quality work. He received neither.

He called me up after the fact. Apologized profusely. Asked if I would be willing to clean up the mess the shyster made of his woods, roads, and landing. We worked out an agreement and I did what I could. But once the soil is down the stream, you can't get it back. The fly-by-night logger went bankrupt. More than once. But he'd get equipment again and go right back at it. When I started out logging, I believed the bad actors—the shady contractors—they would get weeded out. I was naïve. I've seen some so crooked, they couldn't piss a straight hole in the snow.

Chapter 18
Going to Town

Situated within the Town of Hinesburg amongst Lincoln Hill, Hayden Hill, and Texas Hill sits seven hundred acres of land known as the Hinesburg Town Forest. For years it was lightly used by a few hikers and horseback riders, four-wheelers, and dirt bikers. Come fall hunting seasons, it would see its share of hunters. The roads were in terrible shape. Four-wheel-drive vehicles could barely navigate the old town road that snaked from Hayden Hill Road and came out a mile away at the end of Economou Road in Huntington at the town boundary.

Bill Hall gave David Brynn the go-ahead to start me working on it. First thing we did was fix up the washed-out old road for as far as we could afford. Fortunately, the town has a large gravel pit. Unfortunately, it was on the other side of the mountain. Enter Steve Russell, chairman of the Hinesburg Town Forest Committee. Steve was able to persuade the town highway crew to bring in loads of tailings. Tailings are fist-sized rocks that were sorted out when the town was making its road-sanding supply. It was just the ticket for the road, and I spread it with the bucket loader on my tractor.

In the early 1950s, the town had turned about thirty acres of various abandoned farm fields into tree plantations. They planted white pine, red pine, Norway spruce, and tamarack. Steve remembered doing some of the planting when he was a kid. They had to keep telling him "Green-end up, boy!" After they got growing, they were never thinned out, so the plantations were in sad shape. A person would have to be dumber than a second coat of paint to try logging in them.

I started logging in the eastern side of the plantations that summer, accessing it using Economu Road. It was full of spindly tall trees growing thicker than hair on a beaver's ass, which I believe is even thicker than on a boar's. I'd cut a tree and it wouldn't fall. It would lean against its neighbor and I'd have to hook onto it and pull it down. Pine and spruce have a great deal of limbs. Hence, more limbs need to be cut off. Hence, one played-out logger at the end of the day. And there were few trees marked that were of log size. This was Pulp City Central and I was fixing to be the mayor. Pulpwood prices had been flat as a turd and hadn't changed much since my first log job in Williston.

I couldn't resist the challenge. I knew I could make the plantation better. I was fortunate to have David Brynn doing all he could to make the woodlot financially feasible. I won't say profitable, but at least I could pay my bills. David was able to get some government cost-sharing funds to get the first few plantations thinned. I received a stipend per acre when I finished the job, and I got all the pulp and firewood for free. There were still some plantations farther into the forest that weren't accessible without major road work, and these would have to be left for a while. It would turn out to be about twenty years.

I ended up working on the Town Forest for thirty years. It became for me what the Eden woodlot had been for Glenn: a place to go when I didn't have other, more lucrative work. I would brush-hog all the field openings around old homesteads and apple trees every year. Good, hourly paid work that I could count on. Over the years, we would add gates at three access points, with signs and parking. More of the old road would be improved and culverts put in, work paid for by the stumpage I would generate from my harvesting. Eventually, mountain bike trails would crisscross throughout the property, and the Hinesburg Town Forest would become known as one of the premier places in New England to enjoy the sport.

Not all were happy about it. The residents who lived on what was once a dead-end road no longer had tranquil summer days. Weekends of peace and quiet were gone. Now they were filled with carloads of mountain bikers coming and going. When they left the forest, speeding and dust became a problem as they blasted down Economou and Hayden Hill roads. Safety and quality of life for the folks that lived on the roads started to be an issue. I guess there can be too much of a good thing.

In December of 2010, days of rain turned into a heavy, wet snowstorm with high winds that flattened most of the plantations. A friend at the end of Economu Road called me the day after and said I needed to come see what happened. Walking the destruction, I was almost in tears. The damage was mostly confined to the plantations. The natural forest withstood the onslaught. All my years of toil were destroyed in a few hours. I guess no good deed goes unpunished.

Chapter 19
I'll Be Dogged

It came about that I added a new crew member. I arrived home from work one Saturday and Karen had just returned from a trip. She'd gone with my sister to help her pick out a yellow Lab pup. My sister bought the last male, leaving only one puppy; a little girl that was the runt of the litter. Karen couldn't stand to leave her there all by her lonesome, so she bought the little nipper. We named her Amber. Amber-Jean Marie. And she turned into the best log-dog and loyal companion that a man could ask for.

I took a job thinning a couple of firewood lots on Camel's Hump State Park in Duxbury. They were miles up a dead-end road and behind a locked gate. I would spend long days at work with Amber-Jean. Often Julius, her brother, who lived next door at my sister's, would tag along. I wanted to make sure I got a sufficient amount of dog hair on me and embedded in the truck cab. I'd work from daylight cutting and skidding, blocking and splitting, until a cord of wood was loaded. Then deliver it at the end of the day when I dragged my ass out of there. I often got more than a cord split up each day so that once or twice a week, I could deliver two cords in a day. It was a long haul out and many times I wouldn't be home until dark.

Of the two lots I thinned, the second one was about a mile beyond the gate and a hundred yards from where the old road ended at a torn-out bridge over a stream. Beyond the stream and up a hill a hundred yards was an old ramshackle house at the end of a town road. Within a few days of commencing the job, I started to have visitors on the landing whilst I was gone.

I was taught to hunt at an early age. I learned how to read and follow sign too. Hell, I can track like Natty Bumppo and shoot the stink off a skunk at fifty paces. And most mornings I would see sign that somebody had been on my landing. I had my shanty there, and the little side-windows slide open. I'd close them when I left and they'd be opened in the morning. My dad made my wood splitter and my shanty. He designed the two doors on one end of the shanty so they would open to accept the wood splitter where I kept it locked up inside. It looked like somebody was checking out the shanty and my wood splitter.

One Monday, Amber-Jean and I came to work, and my shanty doors were wide open. They had cut the lock with bolt cutters. All I had left was a steel I-beam on wheels. The dirty bastards had come with tools and stole the motor, the hydraulic pump, control valve, and hydraulic cylinder. They'd lugged them off and I had a pretty good idea where. Those parts were heavy. They'd have to make more than one trip or have more than one person. They would leave sign of their passing. Amber-Jean and I started tracking.

I follow their trail down the road and across the stream to that old run-down shack. Nobody was there, and Amber-Jean and I sniffed around, looking for any sign of my splitter parts, but they didn't leave any lying about. Just my luck they wouldn't be quite that stupid. Probably had a buyer lined up before they stole them. We drove back to Jonesville, the nearest public phone, and called the State Police. They sent a trooper out and I told him what I'd found on my tracking mission, and he said he'd check it out. He didn't see much hope of recovering my splitter parts. I never saw those parts or the trooper again. My wood splitter was gone and I'd have to accept it.

My dad had another engine, but I had to pay for another pump, valve, and cylinder. We made the splitter better, stronger, faster, and with a four-way slip-on wedge. It took some time for me to get over the sense of violation a person feels when they're robbed. I can't comprehend people who would choose to steal instead of putting their efforts into an honest job. It must have taken them considerable time and toil to dismantle my wood splitter and carry it down the road, across the stream and up the hill. I hope they popped a nut doing it.

It was after finishing the long haul out of Camels Hump that I decided to sell my one-cord truck and buy one that could deliver a two-cord load. I found one that was almost new, or had been back when I was ten. A blue 1967 Chevrolet C-40 with a twelve-foot-long dump box. It had a tiny little 292 six-cylinder engine. You could fit two mechanics and their toolboxes under the hood to work on it. The top speed was about fifty-five miles per hour, downhill, with a good tailwind. I wasn't in a hurry. I named her Ol' Blue.

Chapter 20
Up Mount Philo the Hard Way

I'd been busting my ass for years now, proving I could do high-quality work removing low-quality wood. It was the spring of the year, and David Brynn was now a state lands forester. He put together a firewood sale on the top of Mount Philo State Park in Addison County. Mount Philo State Park was Vermont's first state park, started back in 1924. There's a mountaintop picnic area with camp sites and stunning views of Lake Champlain, the valley, and the Adirondacks and Green Mountains to the west and south. From September to November, Mount Philo is an excellent viewpoint for migrating raptors, such as kestrels, merlins, and Cooper's and red-tailed hawks. In 1929, the carriage road was improved to allow motor vehicles to access the summit. It's a paved, one-way road that swings up and around one side of the mountain to the summit and then swings down around the other side to take visitors back to the bottom.

Now that I had a larger truck, I thought it would be handy if I used it to move my tractor. I backed the truck up to a bank then drove the tractor off the bank and into the bed of the truck.

With the bucket loader raised up over the truck's cab, the tractor just barely fit. This placed the winch and the rear wheels, which are the heaviest parts of the tractor, to the rear of the truck. And mister man, she was freighted! Since I'm not quite a complete idiot, I used a chain to fasten the dump box down. This was done so it wouldn't go up unexpectedly of its own accord while trucking the tractor.

When I arrived at Mount Philo, I briefly contemplated unloading the tractor at the bottom and driving it up the road to the job site near the summit. I stopped at the parking area and I took a quick gander around but didn't see a decent bank to unload it. Later, under cross-examination by my dad, I admitted that I didn't look really hard. I knew I had a good spot up top. If I unloaded at the bottom, I would have to drive the tractor up to the top and walk all the way back down to get the truck. I was chopping at the bit to get working so I headed up the mountain.

Ol' Blue had a four-speed transmission: Low, first, second, and third gears. First, second, and third could be shifted into, up-and-down, on the go, with ease, while using the clutch. For low gear—what I called "bulldog low," the one needed to start out with a heavy load—the truck and its transmission had to be at a standstill. When in first gear, if it ran out of power, for instance when going up a hill, downshifting into bulldog low could be a bit dicey. The truck either had to stop, or the operator had to time it perfectly and shift it the split second the truck wasn't going forward and wasn't rolling back. It was like trying to time the end of the swing of a pendulum: the timing of the stick shift, clutch, and gas pedal had to be seamless.

I was able to go in second gear for the first part of the road where the climb was gradual, but as I made a hairpin switchback turn, I downshifted into first gear and kept Ol' Blue wound up tighter than a three-day clock. I'd only been up the road once before, riding with David to look at the woodlot, and was a bit foggy on the layout. I should've paid better attention.

I was hammering my way up the mountain when I realized there was a wicked steep grade right in front of me and it was too late to stop and downshift to bulldog low. To be honest, I thought I could make it. There was a wall of ledge on the left side of the road and a damn near sheer drop down the mountain on the right side. And I mean drop, with no guardrails of any sort. Mother of Pearl!

The steepest part is only about forty yards long, and I was praying I'd make it. I felt like I was in the little blue engine that thought it could, thought it could, thought it could. But this one could not, it could not, it could not. The little 292 six-cylinder just didn't have enough moxie in her, and she started lugging down while I was right in the middle of the steepest part of the hill. Well I could've shit a cat turd. Because to sweeten the deal, as I glanced ahead, a park ranger was on the left side of the road, sweeping pine needles off it where they'd built up over the winter. Peachy! He stopped sweeping and stared at me as I realized I was going to have to hit bulldog low, and by God I better not miss it!

I let off the gas pedal that I had glued to the floor as I pushed in the clutch pedal the same distance. Simultaneously, I jammed the stick shift forward into bulldog. It went in with a solid CHUNK! I immediately dumped the clutch back out, hoping it didn't slip, burn, or blow, and feathered the gas pedal a bit before I steadily fed her more. Though the truck hesitated from my shifting, she kept going up the grade.

But that bit of hesitation, along with the badly balanced load of the tractor combined with the steep grade, was too damn much. The laws of physics are absolute and are strictly obeyed. Ol' Blue's front tires started coming off the ground!

Stopping wasn't an option. I'd never hold her on the steep grade, so I kept her tail-walking up the hill. My front wheels were about four feet off the ground as I rode the biggest wheelie of my life past one terrified park ranger. He'd plastered himself to the rock ledge on the side of the road like hair on soap. I only caught a quick glance of him as I drifted by, as my attention was elsewhere. His eyes were bugged out and bigger than saucer plates. The man looked even more scared than I was if that was possible.

I was lucky enough to keep the steering wheel straight through the whole episode, mostly because I was frozen with fear. When I came to the crest of the hill, Ol' Blue came in for a landing and touched down on the tarmac like a two-seat Cessna. I kept right on a-going like nothing happened.

An hour or so later, the park ranger stopped by where I'd begun to clear a spot roadside for my log landing. He introduced himself and we shook hands.

"Did you know your front wheels were way off the ground when you went by me sweeping the road?"

I dead-panned right back at him, serious as a preacher, "Really? No kidding! I didn't notice." I picked up my chainsaw from where I'd set it. "Nice meeting ya. Well, these trees won't cut themselves. I better get back at it."

I slipped my hard hat's face-shield down and turned away so he couldn't see me smile and roll my eyeballs.

Chapter 21
Shooting the Breeze

Over the course of my many years in the woods, I've cleared a number of driveways and building lots. It wasn't long after finishing Mount Philo that I secured a job doing so. It was only a hoot and a holler down the road from my home in West Bolton. Jack Hillary had hundreds of acres and was ready to build a few houses on it. The access right-of-way off the Stage Road was shared with the adjacent landowner, Walt Thompson. For the first twenty yards, it was a shared driveway on Thompson's property, then it forked right and left, the left going to Thompson's house. The right fork went onto Jack's property, where I was to widen the old log road for the driveway to the building lots.

Once I had the trees removed to widen the road, Jack hired a local guy with a backhoe, Duff Barker, to remove stumps and put in a decent roadbed with side ditches and culverts. The road went straight up a gradual grade for about a hundred yards and then turned to the right to a flat area where I cleared a spot to land the wood and later be used as a building lot. I was to clear two more lots beyond the landing as well.

It was soon evident Walt Thompson didn't like that there were going to be houses built next door. He insisted Jack didn't have the right-of-way to use his property. Jack tried to reason with him but he wouldn't listen. Wouldn't believe the facts in the deed. Duff and I would leave our equipment on the landing at the end of each workday. The first trouble occurred when a window in Duff's backhoe cab got a rock thrown through it. He thought Thompson might be the culprit, but there was no way to prove it. Duff and Jack had a heated discussion with Walt, and nothing else happened for a few days. I kept pecking away at the job and minded my own business.

On a Monday morning, Duff noticed one of the eighteen-inch-diameter culverts he'd installed—the one closest to Thompson's house—was packed full of rocks. Duff was able to remove the rocks, but it was a hell of a job, and he was ripping mad. He still had no way to prove who was doing it. But if Walt were a fox, he'd have feathers in his mouth.

Two days later, the culvert was plugged again. This time, there were rocks shoved in it a few feet and then one was used to pound the end of the culvert flat. Duff was so mad he could chew up nails and spit out a barbed wire fence. I was still trying to stay out of it and let Jack and Duff handle the problem, but I couldn't help but wonder if sooner or later, something was going to happen to draw me into the fray.

Duff fixed the culvert, but the next week it was plugged again. I left him working to unplug it and went to cutting trees for the two building lots beyond my landing. At lunch time, I decided to go home to eat and I heard a chainsaw running down by the beginning of the driveway. When I drove down, Duff was there, and had just cut down a sixteen-inch DBH yellow birch that was growing where the road forked. He'd dropped it down the middle of Walt Thompson's driveway. He was standing there grinning like an idiot and I thought it fit perfect.

"There! That ought to teach that stupid son of a bitch! He wants to plug my culverts; I'll plug his driveway!"

Great. Another steaming load of good news. I got out of my truck and walked over.

"Well Duff, that's just dandy. But who's the guy doing all the tree cutting on this here job?"

"Why, you are Bill. But what's that got to do with it? Did you want to drop that birch?" He replied, looking confused, like he didn't quite grasp my question.

"Come on Duff! Who do you think Walt's going to blame for having a tree laying in his driveway when he gets home?"

A look of realization finally seeped in somewhere.

"Oh. I guess I didn't figure on that."

"For Christ sakes, Duff, he's going to come home and see that tree laying there and blame it on me! Then he'll start smashing my equipment too!"

"Well I'm moving my backhoe out of here. I've got another job to do for a couple of weeks."

"The hell you are! You can't just run off and leave me to deal with this mess you've started," I said as I pointed at the tree.

"He started it when he smashed my window and plugged my culverts!"

"I don't care which or whether, Duff! That don't matter now! We've got to come up with some way to put an end to this shit."

So Duff and I came up with an idea. My dad always said if you come up with enough ideas, sooner or later you'll get a good one. This was not one of those times.

Our problem was that we didn't have any hard evidence to prove Walt was doing the damage. But if we could catch him in the act, we'd have him by the short hairs. We could bring the law in and maybe he'd leave us alone.

We figured that when Walt came home and saw the big tree blocking his driveway, he'd go off the deep end. Odds were he'd do exactly like I'd said: he'd take his anger out on my tractor. We would use it for bait. Duff had a VHS camcorder and would film the dirty deed.

We knew Walt got home from work around four-thirty. At four fifteen, I was hiding in the woods near the fork in the driveway where I could watch to see how much Walt enjoyed having a tree in his driveway. Duff was up hiding near my landing on a rocky outcropping that gave him a bird's eye view of my tractor on the landing below, camera at the ready.

At 4:20, Jack Hillary arrived and drove up his new road and out of sight. Balls! This sure puts a fly in the ointment. Duff watched him drive across the landing and out my skid road toward the building lots. Five minutes later, I saw a red Toyota pickup with a man driving and a woman in the passenger side go up Jack's driveway and out of sight. Duff watched them take the same route Jack did. Well this was just ducky!

I sat there wondering what in the hell I should do, when Walt pulled in. He jumped out of his pickup and looked at the tree lying there. I could hear him swearing and thought I saw steam coming out of his ears. There's a metal real estate sign by the side of the road that Jack had put out, and Walt jumped back in his truck, backed up to it, hopped out, and pried it out of the ground. Tossing it in the back of his truck, he jumped back in and tore up Jack's driveway toward my landing. The plot thickened.

I started hotfooting it through the woods toward my landing to stop him before he did too much damage to my tractor, but enough to get some good footage for the six o'clock news. I stopped at the edge of the landing and there was Walt. He had the metal real-estate sign and was wailing the tar out of my tractor with it, swearing like a sailor with each whack. I stepped out of the woods about thirty feet from him.

"That'll do, Walt! Put the sign down and leave my tractor alone!" I was confident Duff was up on the rocks to my right, getting all of this on film.

"We've had enough of you busting our stuff! And this time we got you dead to rights!" I glanced up at the place where Duff was supposed to be filming. Dingleberries! The rock was as empty as last year's bird's nest. No Duff to be seen. When he saw Jack and the red Toyota go through, he abandoned his post and went to find out what was going on.

Walt was mad enough to climb a tree to fight a bear.

"You lousy son of a bitch!" He screamed.

He chucked the metal sign at me, but it was a sad shot, going short and wide, and I didn't even have to move. I think it made him even hotter.

He started coming at me, but I held my ground and said, "Now you hold it right there, Walt! I didn't cut that tree! Duff did! What do you expect after all you've done to him?"

"I don't care if you cut it or not! I'm sick of this shit! I'm going to go get my shotgun and fill you full of lead, you asshole! You just wait!"

He jumped back in his truck and lit out down the driveway, and then I saw him running up to his house.

Well, this can't be good. I checked my tractor for damage, and thankfully, he hadn't hurt it much. I know he told me to wait, but I decided against it. I let out a "Halloo!" and heard an answer from the woods toward the first building lot. I started walking to where my skid road comes onto the landing when two shots rang out, and I had lead whizzing through the trees around me. Holy Crap! The crazy bastard *did* get a shotgun! I sprinted down my skid road, and looking back at the landing, I could see Walt running onto it and stuffing shells into a double-barrel shotgun.

A shotgun can throw a heap of lead. If you get blasted by one you'll be casting a polka dot shadow. I sped up and quit looking behind me. I came up to Jack's truck and the couple's red Toyota. Seems Jack invited them there as prospective buyers for the building lot. The couple were sitting in the truck, Jack and Duff standing alongside it.

"Who's shooting!?" Jack asked.

"It's Walt! He's got a shotgun and he's coming this way. I'm heading that-a-way!" I shouted as I pointed ahead, and I kept right on jogging by. I consider myself a lover, not a fighter, especially when a foaming-at-the-mouth, mad son of a bitch is coming with a double-barrel shotgun. I can't stomach violence, and I've got two legs that aren't partial to it, either. I figured it was every man for himself and let the devil take the hindmost.

"Wait up!" Duff yelled.

I didn't bother to reply and picked up the pace. I glanced behind me, and Duff and Jack were trailing twenty yards back. I figured I didn't have to outrun Walt, just those two. We bounded through the forest like the last of the Mohicans.

We circled around and came out on the Stage Road next to a house and asked to use the phone. Jack called the State Police. Duff called his wife and told her to bring him his .338 deer rifle.

"What the hell are you going to do?!" I asked him.

"I'm not going to let that bastard chase me out of the woods! I'm going back after him!"

"This calls for brains, not bullets, you dumbass!" I was getting irritated. "It ain't worth somebody getting shot over."

The Richmond police got there before his wife did. The patrolman stopped Duff from opening season on Walt. I called Karen out in Westford visiting her family, and I told her to stay out there with our kids until she heard from me. Walt knew where I lived.

We were standing there in the road talking with the Richmond cop when the couple in the red Toyota came driving up. They'd had a good time with Ol' Double Barrel Walt.

When the three of us had beat our hasty retreat, Walt had come running up to their Toyota and poked the muzzle of his shotgun into the guy's window, real personal like. He wanted to know where the logger had gone. I guess I'd pissed him off no end, and he wanted to fill my carcass with hot lead. The guy told him I'd run off and finally talked Walt into lowering his weapon.

It turned out the guy was a private detective and it was just by the grace of God that he didn't have his side-arm with him. He said he would've shot Walt right through the door of his truck. He felt that threatened; was that scared. He said it was nip and tuck for a while, trying to talk Walt off the trigger. For some reason they decided not to purchase a building lot.

A few months later I had to go to court and testify about the whole crazy ordeal. It all seemed senseless. Duff dropping that big yellow birch down Walt's driveway was just about the stupidest thing he could've done. Why I let myself get sucked into the whole mess is something I regret to this day. How did things get so out of control? From the minute Jack had begun trying to build houses on his property, events went cockeyed.

It was clear Walt had anger issues. When things didn't go the way he liked, he only had one way to deal with it, and that was with vandalism and violence. At the court appearance to settle the right-of-way dispute, Walt lost. Then he lost all reasoning. I suppose there are people who can't handle having a bad day—or a bad week or month—and they feel like the whole world is against them. They hit rock bottom and have nowhere to turn. Some do what Walt did and it still fills me with remorse. He climbed into his pickup truck, sat in his driveway and blew his brains out.

Chapter 22
Paying the Dues

Time rolled by as I worked log jobs in Franklin, Chittenden, and Addison counties. Much of the work was on woodlots where I was doing timber stand improvement. TSI means the removal of low-grade trees to allow the better, higher quality trees to prosper. Often I got the material for free, and sometimes I paid the landowner a few dollars per cord. It would vary depending on the accessibility, terrain, and length of skidding distance. Occasionally, I'd have a load of saw logs to sweeten the deal.

There's no trick to doing quality woods work. All it takes is the will to do it—the patience; the dedication. A strong dose of moral fortitude is needed to make good decisions that favor the forest, even when you know doing things right doesn't always mean doing things easy. And especially when you know it might take longer and earn you less money. It can be a hard pill to swallow when the days are long and sixty-hour work weeks are needed to accomplish these goals and still pay the bills.

There is one key necessity a successful logger must have that can't be underestimated, and that's the physical ability needed to labor all day in demanding, unrefined settings and weather conditions. Plus the capacity and drive to get up the next morning and do it all over again. And again. And again. The working discipline needed by the self-employed is driven by the need to succeed. They get paid for what they produce. They can't behave like some unionized employee who does as little as possible, and the easy ones twice, and still receives a paycheck.

Being a one-man-and-a-dog crew, I didn't have the luxury of having a second pair of hands to make certain jobs easier. Like cutting back a gnarly, hairy winch cable and tying a knot in it. Putting chains on the tires of my tractor wasn't a simple process without help. Long pulls of the winch cable would have me busier than a beaver in a sawmill. Cable doesn't come off the drum easy. It has to have some resistance so it won't get snarled. I'd pull what cable I could, walk back to the winch and pull out some more, and walk back and pull again for all I was worth, often trudging through snow, ice, and mud.

Wedging and pushing over trees must be thought out in greater detail when working alone. A technique I used was to reverse the felling procedure by cutting the back cut first. As the back cut was being made, I would drive a felling wedge in behind the chainsaw, keeping the tree from rocking back and pinching the saw bar. Visualization was needed, because I was cutting on the opposite side of the where the directional felling notch would be made. The notch is cut last and must correspond to the back cut by leaving the proper amount of hinge wood and still point the tree in the right direction. Then I could push the tree over with my equipment and have my chainsaw in a safe place. Sometimes I'd have to wedge it over, pounding on multiple wedges with a club if I couldn't get equipment to it. There's something empowering about using a simple tool like a wedge and my physical strength to bring a tree that weighed thousands of pounds to the forest floor.

Working alone taught me patience and problem-solving and thinking ahead. If I got my chainsaw bound in the back cut, and the tree needed to be pushed over, who was going to grab my chainsaw when the tree started to go so it wouldn't get smashed to smithereens? Amber-Jean? I wouldn't put it past her. She helped in many intangible ways.

There were times when working on a back-road landing and the equipment would be shut down that the quiet peacefulness of the forest would gather around Amber-Jean and me as she lay at my feet while I filed my saw. Times when I'd be sitting on a log and swigging from a water jug and A.J. Marie would hop up and walk down the log and lick me on the jaw. I'd pour a gulp of water in my hand, and she'd lap and drool till it was gone and give me a "thank you" lick. Occasions when we'd walk together up my skid roads with a shovel at the end of a long day to check water bars if rain was in the forecast. Having her by my side made the task seem like a stroll, a walk with my log-dog.

On hot summer days, I would often take a twenty-minute power nap after lunch. I'd find a comfy spot in the shade, throw an old blanket down, and wad up a sweatshirt for a pillow. A.J. would doze beside me and keep an eye out for interlopers. I'd wake up refreshed and raring to go for an afternoon of thrashing.

And heaven help the guy who tried to get in my shanty if Amber-Jean Marie was on duty. Visitors learned to leave a note on the shanty door rather than risk life and limb to try and put it inside. She wouldn't make a sound until the door was opened, then she'd be coming for you. But she was the best around my young daughters. They'd play dress-up with her and she'd go along, happy as a clam.

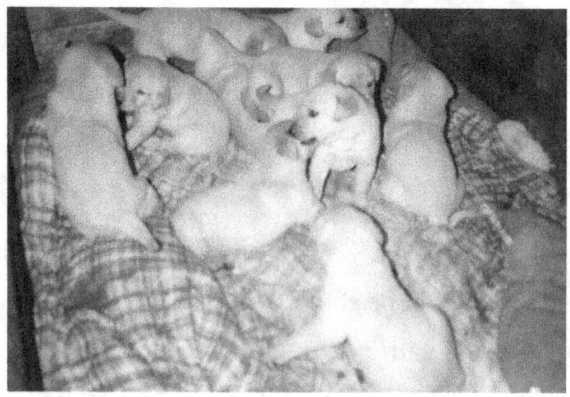

She was a topnotch mother too. I midwifed her through two litters of purebred pups. Ten each time. We never lost a one.

And when it came to retrieving ducks and geese, she had the heart of a lion. On nasty days in the fall when it was too windy and rainy to work, A.J. and I would hunt the various beaver swamps I knew from my travels logging.

Karen frowned on me spending too many days hunting, so A.J. and I had to keep it on the down-low. I'd sneak out hunting gear and clothes and stash them in the truck, and on the way home I'd give away to friends any game I'd taken. I always kept a gun in the truck's rear window gun rack, and a bag of sawdust behind the seat that I'd sprinkle on my clothes before I went in the house to really sell it. I'd even give Amber-Jean a rub down with it to get the smell of the swamp off her. It was a secret shared between a man and his dog, and A.J. never squealed. Once Karen did ask why Amber was so tired if all she did was sleep in the shanty all day.

It was rewarding being in the forest and able to do work that improved its productivity. Over time I came to realize that it would be to my benefit to be able to offer road and trail improvements to complement my ability to manage woodlots. I decided I would purchase a bulldozer to enable me to do so, knowing I could also use it to skid timber if I continued to keep my skidding distances reasonably short.

I'd always thought, and still do, that the John Deere 450C bulldozer is one of the best for working in the woods. I began searching for a used 450C and knew where to look: out of state. I wanted one that had never seen any use in the woods of Vermont, or woods anywhere. It's rougher than hell on them. I looked for one used to push dirt on construction sites.

I found a beauty in New Haven, Connecticut. It was a 1980, used by a large construction company to finish up around foundations after the main work was done by a larger dozer. I got a Small Business Administration loan for sixteen thousand dollars and brought it home. I went all through it and put new sprockets, rollers, tracks, and grouser pads on it. After I installed a used winch and limb risers, I was ready to hit the woods. It turned out to be one of the best investments I ever made, and I kept it for the duration of my career.

I had my tractor paid off and still in good shape. My firewood truck was paid for, too, though it's damn near an antique. I get paid just as much for wood Ol' Blue delivers as I would using a shiny new truck with a big monthly payment. Dad and I kept her toggled together. He could fix anything but a broken heart or the crack of dawn. The bulldozer payment wasn't too steep, though I still carried job liability and truck insurance, and the SBA loan required me to have insurance on the bulldozer as well. Insurance might be the biggest racket going, next to loan-sharking.

Chapter 23
"A Man's Got to Know His Limitations"

Clint Eastwood's Dirty Harry spoke this famous line many years ago in the 1973 movie *Magnum Force*. I was only sixteen at the time, and Mom wouldn't let me go to R-rated movies. Too bad. Maybe if I had heard that sage wisdom, I wouldn't have tried to replace the wheel bearing on Ol' Blue.

I'd never fixed wheel bearings before, but how hard could it be? I was only doing the rear one on the driver's side. I pulled the tires and hub off and tore into it. I put the new ones on and snugged up the big castle nut on the axle good and tight, packed it with wheel bearing grease, and put her back together. Oops! Nobody told me I was supposed to tighten up the big castle nut and then back it off half a turn.

Now that I had the bulldozer, I was trying to increase production, and I'd have Dicky Streeter help me when he could. The morning with the new wheel bearing, Dicky, Amber-Jean and I were rolling down the Richmond-Hinesburg Road on our way to work. As I made the corner heading toward the top of Mechanicsville Hill, something didn't feel right with the truck.

I pulled over at the top of the hill and hopped out. I put my hand on the rear hub I'd just fixed and you could fry an egg on it. I hopped back in and told Dicky what I'd found.

"Let's drive down to Iroquois Manufacturing's parking lot and check it out." I said. "I have a friend, who works there."

Mechanicsville Hill is about half a mile long as it snakes down to the four corners at CVU High School. Iroquois Manufacturing was about halfway down.

I pulled back onto the road, and when I shifted from first to second gear, second gear was gone! I got nothing! It was like the whole stick shift was in neutral! I was going about fifteen miles per hour and hadn't started down the main hill yet, but we were on a slight downhill slope, coasting along.

"Holy shit, Dick! No gears!" And I tromped down on the brake pedal. It went right to the floor!

"No brakes! I've got nothing!" as I furiously pumped the brake pedal three or four times. We're rolling for the crest of the hill!

"The emergency brake!" Dicky yelled.

The emergency brake on Ol' Blue was this cantilevered lever sticking out of the floorboards in front of the bench seat between Dicky and me. The premise was that when it was pulled up, straightened out, and locked into place, it would tighten a brake band around the truck's drive shaft and lock it down. It didn't work for beans when the truck was parked. It wouldn't slow Ol' Blue down if she was going one mile every two weeks. At the speed we were going, there wasn't a chance in hell of it working. But Dicky started pumping it up and down like a thirsty man on a dry well. Or like his life depended on it—hard to say.

I glanced in my side-view mirror and saw the rear tires were sticking out about a foot farther than they normally did. Well, don't that take the fuzz off the peach! The whole axle had walked its way out of the banjo housing. Brake fluid was spraying out the busted brake line, which had torn off because I kept trying the brakes hoping they might be healed by an act of God. We coasted over the crest and began to pick up speed going down the first run of the hill. I got this sickening, helpless feeling, and it was déjà vu all over again: the Bolton Notch Sleigh Ride Part Two.

"What the hell should I do?! There's no place to go! Son of a bitch!" I yelled as we hit the bottom of the first hill and cruised along a flat spot, then shot across a bridge. Ol' Blue's steering wheel was shaking like it was having a seizure.

"Just keep us on the goddamn road! Look for a place to ditch it!" Dicky shouted.

We made it through a left-hand corner around a chunk of ledge, and then we were eyeballing a long, straight, downhill pitch. Mother! We zipped past Iroquois Manufacturing, past houses on both sides of the road, mailboxes, road signs, driveway culverts, cars parked in driveways. We were both frantically scanning ahead, but there was no time to see anything before we went whizzing by it. And now we'd built up a head of steam like a runaway train.

"We'll never make the turn at the bottom!"

"I don't believe this shit is happening again! Goddamn it, Torrey!" Why Dicky pointed out the obvious in what could well be our last minutes I have no idea. Maybe he wanted to be sure he got it on the record.

Ol' Blue didn't have anything in the cab for Dicky to hold onto. Amber-Jean was on the seat between us, and Dicky had his left arm around her and his right arm braced on the dash. I had the steering wheel in a death grip as I tried to keep control while we plummeted down the hill.

We were a blue streak, both inside and out, as Dicky and I continued to cuss avidly, heading into a hard left turn doing about fifty! The rear axle had come out even more, and I couldn't keep her from sliding. The right rear end came around and we went sideways across both lanes to the left side of the road, onto a guy's lawn and headed for his house.

Some would say what happened next was just shit luck. I don't. I think it was the gods of the woods, looking down on their wayward disciple in his time of need. Call it what you will. I've turned a lot of trees into stumps and now a stump came to my rescue. It was an eight-inch-diameter elm on the guy's lawn, and the truck's passenger-side front tire hit it as we were sliding sideways. It turned Ol' Blue ninety degrees and slowed us down drastically. Now we're going at a tenth of the speed we had been, but backwards!

When we hit the stump and spun to the side, it gave us quite a jolt. Dicky got pitched against the door, rapped the door handle, and out he went, along with Amber-Jean. They hit the lawn and rolled out of sight, leaving me flying solo, steering with my side mirrors as I barely missed the guy's bay window. Somehow, Dicky's door closed shut when they jettisoned; otherwise the bay window would've torn it clean off. There was a car parked in the driveway and I was headed right at it! I cranked the wheel just in time to miss it by a couple inches, then cranked it back the other way as I turned Ol' Blue to the side of the house and headed for the backyard. It had an uphill pitch and Ol' Blue finally came to a halt.

I hopped out, resisted the urge to kiss the ground, and ran back to see if everybody was all right. A.J. came running up to me and I grabbed her by the collar. Dicky was okay, too, though both he and Amber-Jean looked a little pale. When Dicky and Amber-Jean flew out the door, a toolbox on the floor followed them, scattering tools from hell to breakfast, with some in the middle of the road. When no cars were coming, I walked out and picked them up, and was walking back when a State Police cruiser came driving by. I gave him a friendly wave and a smile. He waved back.

The guy who owned the house came out and wasn't even upset. Said his house had been hit a couple of times over the years. He let me use his phone and I called a tow truck. He got a rake and shovel and we fixed up his lawn. O'l Blue took some fixing up, too, and once done, I sold her. I decided to go back to a one cord truck. The weight of a newer, two-cord truck would put it into a class where I would need a commercial driver's license. I didn't want to go through all the happy horse shit required for a CDL. I found a used Dodge Ram one-ton truck with a nice dump box all set up for hauling wood. It was four-wheel drive with a Cummins diesel engine. Sweet! I was happier than a skinny flea on a fat dog.

Art got a charge out of my episode down Mechanicsville Hill. We were still close buddies. Starting families and raising kids had created demands on our time and energy. Fall would always find us in deer camp where we'd reconnect and be back together in the woods we loved. I'd trade him firewood in return for his help in the woods or on a construction project I had at home. It was in his early thirties that he was diagnosed with Crohn's disease. He never complained about it. No "Woe is me" from Art, even when he had to undergo surgery. The man was tougher than wang leather. His father-in-law owned a woodlot in Underhill on the old town Dump Road and was looking for a logger. Art got me the job.

Chapter 24
Answering the Bell

Dump Road was a two-mile-long, abandoned stretch that went between one town road and another. It was in rough shape and took a four-wheel-drive rig to make it through. I improved it for the half-mile section to the woodlot to get a log truck to it. I cleared a landing and hauled in my shanty. It was late fall and I planned to be there all winter. I would be needing my logging headquarters. Winters working in the woods always passed better with the shanty on-site. I even had a battery-operated TV now. I could catch the end of *The Price is Right* and watch the weather at noon while toasting my sandwich, I'd be all warmed up and ready to go for the afternoon portion of pounding down trees.

I no longer locked my shanty since those rat bastards stole my wood splitter. I never kept my wood splitter in the shanty anymore either. I'd found out when they came with bolt cutters that a lock wasn't going to stop a thief. What I did was put a sign on the door of the shanty that said: "Welcome to use it, but please don't abuse it." Trust in our fellow man has to start somewhere. I believe that trusting everybody and trusting nobody are equal failings. But if I ever caught somebody stealing, they'd best hope their soul's with Jesus, because their ass would be mine.

Within the first week, I started having unwanted visitors on my landing over the weekends. I'd come to work on a Monday and see signs of yahoos being there. They would spin in circles, doing donuts with their trucks on my landing. They left beer cans in the shanty and shot up liquor bottles on my log pile. They busted off an old guy's mailbox back on the town road, brought it to my shanty, and nailed it to the side of it. They had about as much common sense as God gave gravel.

One Monday I came to work, and the shanty doors were wide open. Everything in the shanty was scattered around the landing. The few tools I kept in it were gone, chucked out into the snow. All my chairs were busted, my radio and TV were smashed. They even broke my broom and dustpan. And then I discovered they'd broken all the gauges on my equipment.

Well, I was madder than a barefoot hornet on a hot rock. Logging is a tough, demanding, difficult way to make a living.

This senseless destruction of my hard-earned possessions really dropped a rusty bucket down my well. I called the State Police and they sent out a trooper. He was very sympathetic, but sympathy was about all he could offer. He said he'd do what he could, but they were spread pretty thin. We stood in front of the shanty discussing the situation.

"Even if we caught 'em, they'd just get a slap on the wrist," he said.

Then he sort of gave me a knowing look and said, "If I were you Mr. Torrey, I'd take care of this problem yourself."

Well, that was just what I was thinking! If I could catch those jerks, I wouldn't slap them on the wrist. I'd slap them into next week looking both ways for Sunday. The visits always seemed to occur on the weekends. Usually Saturday nights. The next Saturday morning, before I left for work, I told Karen I wouldn't be home that night because I was going to sleep in the shanty. I didn't tell her all I was thinking, because I didn't want her to worry. Fact was, I wasn't going to sleep in the shanty, for a couple of reasons. The first was that I didn't like the feeling of being boxed in or surrounded in the shanty. The second reason was I didn't want to scare them off. I wanted to catch these assholes.

I worked all day in the snow-covered woods, then prepared my supper in the warm comfort of the shanty. I sat thinking, alone in the quiet, the fire crackling in the little stove, the smell of wet mittens and fragrant sawdust mingling with the wholesome aroma of my meal. I kept the woodstove's door open and watched the dancing flames cast flickering shadows around me, but I had a queasiness in the pit of my stomach that wasn't from my cooking; a tightness in my body that wasn't caused by my labors of the day. I was afraid. Afraid of what might unfold in the coming night. Not many aren't when they know danger might lay ahead. I knew the real test would be finding the courage despite the fear.

I studied on how to handle different scenarios the night could bring. I had to try to stop these morons. It was my livelihood at stake. I had a family to support, bills to pay. If I missed a day or two of production, it could mean no logs would go to the mill that week. The trucker wouldn't come for half a load—he got paid by how much was on his truck. No load, no paycheck. Time and money spent replacing broken gauges was the same as if they'd stolen food from my family. Would they burn my shanty next? Torch my equipment? It may be fun and games to them, but to me it was my life's work.

I set my trap. I backed my truck up the skid road about fifty yards, to where it made a slight turn into some hemlock trees. From my truck's cab I could see the shanty and the entrance to the landing, and hopefully they wouldn't see me. I knew I wouldn't be able to stay awake all night. Working in the cold winter woods always made me sleepy, and I didn't want to doze off and miss the festivities. I had a remedy. I took a big spool of heavy monofilament fishing line and tied it to a tree on the side of the driveway coming onto the landing. I strung it across the entrance and around through the woods to my truck's driver side mirror and put a little bell on it.

As I settled in my truck for the night, I had a camera, a baseball bat, and, tucked in a shoulder holster under my coat, my revolver. I hoped the hell I wouldn't need it. I knew from the sign on the landing what to expect. I was going to be outnumbered, and sure as a fat dog farts, they'd have firearms and be liquored up. Always a great combination. I decided if it came down to gun play, I'd rather be judged by twelve than carried by six.

I think I dozed off around nine o'clock. At midnight I was jolted awake by the bell ringing on the mirror beside me. There were headlights on the landing! I pounced out of my truck and sprinted for the shanty, camera in one hand, baseball bat in the other.

I'll be a monkey's bare-assed uncle! It was the State Police. I gave that trooper quite a start. When I explained what I was doing, he looked at me like my antenna wasn't picking up all the channels. He got in his cruiser, smiled, shook his head and said, "Happy hunting, Mr. Torrey."

I stood there alone in the frigid winter woods, stars winking through the bare branches as a half-moon hung close enough to knock it down with a stick. I breathed a sigh of relief as I watched the red glow of his taillights twinkle and fade down the truck road. I decided to head for home too. Late as it was, they probably wouldn't show up now anyhow.

It might be thought that what I did was all for naught and my winter's night watch was a failure. I don't. A lot of people back in those days had police radio scanners. Especially the low-lifes who were trying to avoid the police. A few days after my midnight meeting, I stopped at the Underhill General Store on my way to work. The storekeeper was talking with a few customers at the counter. I heard them say the scuttlebutt around town was, "Don't screw with that logger up on the old dump road. He's a crazy bastard." I never had any unwanted visitors for the rest of the winter.

Chapter 25
The Waterworks

My reputation as a trustworthy logger with years of experience in the woods was beginning to bear fruit. One evening I received a phone call from Charlie Grant, a logger who lived in New Haven. He'd gotten a log job at the defunct 664-acre Waterworks of the City of Vergennes located in Bristol. He made me an offer I couldn't refuse. I could make as much in a week as I was making now and not have the headache of fixing equipment if it broke, paying the repair bill, buying fuel, and keeping woodlots lined up. He wanted me because of my reputation as a person who knew how to do things right in the woods. I made it clear before I accepted the position that I wouldn't take shortcuts. I would do the work in the forest to my satisfaction. Charlie readily agreed.

He was older than me but had only been working in the woods for about five years. He owned a 225 Timberjack skidder, a John Deere 450C bulldozer, and a log truck with a good, reliable driver—all that was needed to do an orderly job in the woods and get the logs to the mill.

The first day with Charlie gave me an awareness of his skidder-driving capabilities. We were cutting in a stand of hemlock on the backside of the pond at the Waterworks. I had a monster of a hemlock notched and my felling wedges tapped into the back cut. All I needed was for Charlie to come in and nudge it over with the skidder, as the bulldozer was under repair and wasn't on the job yet. When Charlie drove in on the skidder, I stopped him and explained what I needed done.

"You see that big hemlock over there? Turn around and use the top of the log arch to push it over. Do it slow and easy. I've got it on a hair trigger."

"I'll push it with the blade."

"No, use the log arch. It's taller. That's a big tree. Better leverage."

"I can get it with the blade."

"I'd use the log arch but suit yourself," I said, but I'm thinking the guy's got no patience. He's going to drive over and push it with the blade because he doesn't want to take the time to turn around and do it with the arch. He isn't thinking ahead. He'll have to turn around anyway after he pushes it so he can hook onto it and skid it. I took my chainsaw and got a good tree length away to watch the show.

The log arch of a skidder is several feet higher than the decking blade. It always does the job easier when it's used. The top of the log arch is fairly narrow. Sometimes the skidder's ass end can't be maneuvered into the proper position to push the tree in the right direction. It could be because of a tree, rock, or stump in the way. That's when the blade can be used as the second option. It wasn't the case here.

When a tree needs to be pushed over, the procedure to do it safely takes a few seconds of patience. When the initial contact is made between the tree and the skidder, it should be only that; contact. Then the operator should very slowly push on the tree. This is because when the tree is moved an inch where the contact is made, the top of the tree, way the hell up in the air, is moving considerably more. This is a lot of weight and momentum to get moving, and it's all pivoting on a thin strip of hinge wood on the stump. Going slow and easy lets the hinge do its job.

Hemlock is twenty ounces to the pound. Pushing a huge one like this, if I'd left too much hinge wood, the skidder couldn't push it. Hence the thin hinge I'd left, or what I called a hair trigger. It needed to be pushed delicately. Charlie did it about as delicate as a bear on a beachball. He drove the skidder up to the hemlock and didn't hardly slow down. He plowed right into it like it was in his way. He broke the hinge and shoved the tree right off the stump. Great Hairy Balls of the gods!

Now the tree could go anywhere, and it decided to fall straight back on the skidder. Thank God the skidder's canopy held up, because the tree landed on top of it with the butt sticking out past the blade and the top end pointed toward the rear end over the log arch. It looked like he'd strapped a huge Christmas tree on the skidder and was taking it home for decorating. Ho! Ho! Ho! I could see this was going to be a merry ol' time working with Charlie! At least he'd be fun to watch.

Charlie had his own log truck too, but thankfully, he didn't drive it. He couldn't drive a hen off a nest. Trucking logs is a necessary evil. I wouldn't take a log truck if you gave me one.

The upkeep is nonstop. Fuel cost and fuel taxes, insurance and registration, and overweight permits make for an expensive vehicle. Keeping current on the CDL rules for the driver is harder than Chinese algebra. The only way to end up with a million dollars from trucking logs is if you started with three.

But logs must get to the mill for money to change hands. Therefore trucking is a vital link. Jerry, Charlie's truck driver, was more like the Missing Link. I think a person has to be a little crazy and a bit brave to drive a log truck. Jerry was all that. And he sure could drive. He could operate the cherry picker loader like it was an extension of his hand: pick the hat right off your head.

The Waterworks had high-quality hardwood on the ridges. It was a mix of red oak and rock maple with a smattering of black birch, red maple, ash, and beech. Down in the valley, along the main water course that fed the pond, was where the white pine really took ahold. Humongous pine with five hundred to a thousand board feet per tree was common. There was also a section of planted red pine in an area near the pond.

Charlie was no fool when he sought me out. The skill and knowledge I drew upon to remove the large, valuable timber was tested constantly. I'd call Art on the phone some evenings after thrashing all day on the Waterworks cutting pine. I'd get his opinion, maybe some pointers that I'd forgotten. Told him my troubles, shared my accomplishments. Asked how he was faring with his tussle with the Crohn's. We both needed a sympathetic ear and we were always there for each other, hell or high water.

The pines were so large they had to be cut in half to bunch them. In order not to waste wood, I measured them into logs and cut them in two pieces at the appropriate spot. Starting from the butt, they would go something like this: two sixteen-foot logs, a fourteen footer, a couple of twelves, and a ten-foot top log. That totals eighty feet. And probably another thirty feet that stayed on the ground where it fell. We weren't taking pulpwood.

Laying down a tree of that length was a challenge that greeted me day after day for weeks on end. Working among the ravines feeding down to the watershed took constant planning and patience. If I dropped a lengthy tree across or down into a ravine or gully at the wrong angle, the brittle pine would break. In a matter of minutes I could ruin a beautiful tree that had spent a century growing to maturity.

When we worked the ridges, I spent my days scrambling up rocky side banks with my chainsaw and wedges to a magnificent red oak or rock maple—a tree that had been stubbornly standing lookout over the ridge, gallantly providing the clean, pure air that I was breathing to climb up to it. I often hugged it, embraced it with both arms. It was a sincere and sobering act. I'd feel its strength. I'd admire its majesty, marvel at its immense crown that reached to the summit of the forest canopy, subordinate to no neighbor. Then I would plan its path to the ground. The first step on its journey to another life serving in a role that seemed a demotion to the one it carried out so loyally for so long on the ridge.

It wasn't called the Waterworks for nothing. There were springs bubbling up all over. And where there's lots of water, there're lots of bugs. I'd become very tolerant of biting pests from years of working in the woods, but these insects were fierce. Early morning would be thick with no-see-ums. They'd burn off around nine and be replaced by clouds of black flies. Eventually, they'd be driven off by swarms of mosquitoes along with deer flies big enough to rape a chicken. Lines would form. Fights would break out.

The electromagnetic field a running chainsaw generated, as well as the exhaust, helped to keep them somewhat at bay. But when I shut it off to fuel up or stopped to file my chain, they were on me like stink on a monkey. At the end of the day, I didn't walk out of the woods, I ran. Or I could let the deer flies carry me out. If I walked briskly backwards, I could clap my hands together and get two or three each time. It was satisfying, but futile. Like shoveling sand against the tide.

Chapter 26
Mad River Glen- Log It If You Can

The Waterworks wasn't the only job Charlie was able to obtain. He got the timber contract to cut on Betsy Pratt's property around Mad River Glen ski area. I only met Betsy once. She was an eccentric old girl who smoked a corn cob pipe. Her dad was the Pratt part of the Pratt & Whitney Company, which made airplane engines. She had land holdings on the hardwood ridges below the ski area, and they hadn't been logged for some time. Probably because nobody was crazy enough.

In the year I'd been working with Charlie, I'd applied what I'd learned from Art about running a bulldozer in the woods. Charlie was driving skidder and cutting up hitches on the landing. I was now a one-man cutting and bunching crew using his 450C dozer. I had to lay off Amber Jean when I took the job with Charlie. Working alone felling huge timber on the Waterworks taught me even more patience when making decisions to remove trees from all kinds of terrain. The big pine trees on the lower ground of the Waterworks had been easier to remove than the large hardwood on the ridges. One or two pine trees cut in half was all the Timberjack skidder could handle. They never had to be bunched far, either, because the terrain the pines were growing on was easier for the skidder.

But dropping large oak, maple, and birch, with crowns that seemed to blossom out like the cap of a mushroom, proved a daring challenge. Hardwood trees on ridges must be felled directionally and bunched with the dozer to where the skidder can hook on and go without getting flipped over. And uphill skids are to be avoided whenever possible. It's sometimes necessary to bunch trees uphill with the dozer for a short distance to the crest of a hill or get them onto a shelf so the skidder can have a downhill pull from there. It's time-consuming and load-limiting to skid trees uphill as a regular practice with the skidder.

Mad River Glen was some of the most challenging terrain to log that I would ever face in my woods career. The old roads were eroded stream beds and faint, horse-road traces, and had to be widened before the Timberjack could scratch its way up the mountain. I did road work that was thrilling all in itself. I'd be nudging rocks half the size of the bulldozer over the edge of the road. They crashed their way down the mountain as I watched, perched in my seat. It was almost straight down in places, and they would soon pitch out of sight, their paths still discernable by the violent shaking of treetops as they bounced off. Like a giant game of Plinko, the bigger ones would ricochet to the bottom. One made it all the way to the field we were landing the logs in. It stopped a few yards short of my car and was almost as big. Could the mountain have been trying to fight back? Give a subtle warning that there are consequences to our actions we might not know of until it's too late?

But there was maple in them-there hills. rock maple selling for a dollar or better a board foot. Betsy Pratt had kept the loggers out for years, and there was some nice, mature timber and a top-dollar price to be had. Some of the best were the hardest to get, but when just one tree can bring hundreds of dollars, it makes them worth fighting for. Some days felt like I'd gone ten rounds in the ring. Bare-knuckled.

The mature maples clinging to those rock-strewn mountainsides would fill anybody with awe. They were even more intimidating to me as I wrapped my arms around them, my hands nowhere near touching. Some would stretch for nigh onto thirty feet or better without a pimple on the bark. They had a presence. I knew I was about to alter something that had been decades in the making. I had an emotional feeling that wasn't quite regret but was bordering near it. But there was also the anticipation of a daunting challenge. Could this be done? And I was in this quest alone with just my sharp saw and the faithful 450C. It was a deadly test of my wits and wisdom, might and muscle, gathered and forged together from my past.

It wasn't like I hadn't worked steep ground before. Art and I had done more than our fair share of mountain goat terrain. I knew from days working sidehills that getting as much timber as possible from above was most always preferable to working it from below. Staggering through the limbs and tops of trees from below while pulling cable and choker uphill gets old quick. And when pulling logs downhill toward the bulldozer, they could get going out of control, or go on the wrong side of trees for the winch cable and have to be re-hooked. Or my favorite: come barreling at the bulldozer like a super-sized battering ram. That really gets your attention.

One practice Art and I had perfected on steep terrain was to hook onto the tree to be cut before I sent it flying down the mountain. This prevented it from ending up in a spot that couldn't be reached with the winch cable. First, get the ass end of the dozer behind a good anchor, be it a stump, tree, or hunk of rock or ledge. Place the choker chain around the tree a couple feet above where the back cut would be, then attach the winch cable, tightening it up, but leaving a bit of slack so it drooped a little. This slack would allow the tree to fall enough to break the hinge wood.

When the back cut is finished, turn and leave on the chosen escape path. Once the tree had fallen almost ninety degrees from straight up, and the hinge wood was mostly broken, Art would give the dozer engine full power and winch in. This would pull the butt off the stump and toward the dozer and get the tree coming to it. Then the tree could be held with the winch brake while being limbed out and topped off without it taking off down the mountain.

But now at Mad River, I was Art-less. My first task each day was to figure out my starting point. I would walk the mountainside of the area I would be working to determine the lowest tree to be cut and bunched to our topside skid road. Usually, we'd already gotten what trees we could from below, and I had some holes in the forest canopy I could use for the upper trees to land in. Trees of the size I was cutting were going to the ground when cut. If other trees got in their way, they wouldn't be for long. I had to place them perfectly.

Once I chose my first victim, I'd get one of the bulldozer's tracks behind something substantial, offset enough to still allow access to the winch. I'd pull cable and lug choker down to the tree to be cut. Sometimes I would use all hundred feet of cable on the winch drum, plus eight-foot chokers tied together. I'd put the choker around the tree and hook it to the winch cable, then scrabble back to the dozer and take up most of the slack in the cable. I'd leave just enough slack for it to break the hinge wood, but not let it go off the stump.

I'd grab my chainsaw, climb back down to the tree, and find and clear an escape route—one that wouldn't just get me away from the tree, but also far enough away from the winch cable if the worst should happen and it, or a choker, snapped. A flying cable could lop off an arm or leg or possibly cut me in half. Steel choker shrapnel could kill me just as dead as a falling tree.

I'd gather all my wits, think things through one last time, and fire up my chainsaw. I'd drop the tree and run, glancing up and moving as quick as I could without panicking. And it was hard not to panic when forces I'd released were shaking the ground. Sometimes the bulldozer would almost stand right on its tail, the front blade pointed skyward even though it was resting on the ground just moments before.

When my heart stopped pounding, I'd walk back to the enormous tree, hung on the mountainside by this thin steel cable, and soak in the enormity of what I'd just done—that a puny man such as I had vanquished a huge denizen of the north woods. One that sprouted up here long before I ever existed. I knew it would live on as a wood product, but where? Most of the logs Charlie sold were exported. I'd never know what would become of these trees. Would the people who purchased the wood feel the same gratitude I felt when I saw the tree standing tall in the forest? Would they ever appreciate what it endured before it was subjugated to man's material needs? Could they comprehend the brutal winters, the thundering rainstorms pounding down, gale-force winds trying to tear it off the mountain throughout its long, courageous life? They would never be aware of the struggle for survival that it fought so gallantly for so long. Would they even have a smidgen of a thought about what occurred to enable them to possess a piece of wood from these mighty trees?

Occasionally I would intentionally lean a tree into a close, downhill neighbor, but I emphasize *lean*. It wouldn't smack into it with force, just gently rest against it. I could then hook onto it with a roll hitch and get it down without the dangerous excitement of launching it down the mountain. But it was often so steep that when I rolled it off, it would make the dozer do a standing ovation, with me on it. I got jerked around so much on the bulldozer on a daily basis I should've changed my name to Bolt Upright.

I used every trick I could muster at Mad River Glen to get the job done and stay in one piece. Charlie wasn't as knowledgeable, or as patient, as I. One Saturday, he got a taste of Mad River logging that wasn't all that palatable. I had the day off and he decided to work by himself. He backed the skidder to the edge of a shelf and pulled the cable down to a big maple, then put a choker on it and snugged up the slack. The only thing he did to anchor the skidder was to put hydraulic down-pressure on the front decking blade. Big mistake. When he cut the tree, it yanked the skidder down the mountain. It barely missed running him over as it came tearing past him and stopped when it smacked into a tree. It was so steep it couldn't climb back up, and he had a hell of a time pulling it up with the bulldozer by himself. He could only run one piece of equipment at a time. And sometimes, even that could be a struggle.

One day at Mad River, Charlie headed off down the mountain with a hitch, and shortly thereafter, he came walking up to where I was cutting and bunching. This usually meant something on the skidder was broken or he was stuck. Considering it was a downhill pitch to the landing, I didn't think he could get stuck.

"Can you bring your saw and come help me? I'm stuck." On a new spur road, he chose to get to the main skid road by turning between some trees, and he made too tight a turn and caught the tail end of the hitch behind a tree. He had released the winch with the hope of getting enough slack to pull the hitch past the tree, but he had no room to maneuver the skidder. Somehow, he had gotten the butt end of a tree from the hitch—a white birch—to slip down below and outside of the skidder apron and become wedged between it and the tire. He couldn't move the skidder forward or back, and things were bound up tight. It's a wonder he didn't tear the tire off the rim.

"Son of a bitch, Charlie! How in the hell did you manage to do that? I ought a put a knot in your head a Boy Scout couldn't get out."

"I thought I could get through there and onto the skid road," he replied.

"Christ, Charlie, you ain't driving a VW. You should've pulled them down through there on a better angle. That was how I had them bunched to go out," I said as I pointed out the longer way he should've gone if he hadn't been in such an all-fired hurry.

I surveyed the situation for a good ten minutes trying to figure out how to make a cut somewhere on the white birch that wouldn't get me killed or in the hospital. I decided where I would cut the man-killer. I had a good feeling that I knew which way the tension on it was, and I could use the rear tire to sort of shield me as it came blasting out of there.

Making the first undercut was the trickiest and most dangerous. I got it done and took a deep breath before commencing to cut the front-side top of the birch. I had a good stance with the saw extended as far as I could to keep my distance, knowing the tree would most likely swing out and away from me. I was totally focused on the job at hand when the birch let go with a loud "POW!" It came out from under there like a white-barked rocket. It damn near took the saw out of my hands as it shot a good fifteen feet away from the skidder and missed hitting Charlie in the chest by about a foot as he stood there gawking. It would've nailed him if another tree hadn't stopped its progress.

I ran over to him, cussing mad. He was about as white as the bark on the birch. "Goddamn, it Charlie! What in the hell were you standing there for?! This ain't no spectator sport!"

He was too scared to say anything as I took my saw and headed back to work. Not scared of me. Scared because he realized he had almost made a fatal mistake by just standing around.

He didn't realize he was even in danger until it was too late. And that can be the nature of the job of logging in the north woods.

I had some good times working with Charlie. He was a good, honest man. We would play practical jokes on each other to break up the hard day's work. I stuffed his lunch bucket with deer turds. He carefully put little wood wedges around my car's tires where I had it parked in the grass, and I sat there spinning when I tried to tear out for home. He got me good on that one. I greased his hard hat headband. Touché. It was all good-natured fun. After a couple years, I felt the urge to be back on my own, and we amicably parted ways.

Chapter 27
Shear Genius

It sure felt good to be working on my own log jobs again. I liked the fact that I was the one who called all the shots. Sure, the work is hard, and the days can be long. Whoever said, If you do what you love you'll never work a day in your life," damn sure didn't work as a logger. But if being able and willing to do hard work isn't considered a skill, it's the sweaty cousin next to it. Some days would have obstacles that were challenging to solve. But like a batter coming to the plate, I stepped up and kept swinging at the pitches I was thrown. I enjoyed the responsibility of having the health and well-being of the forest in my hands. I took an enormous amount of pride and pleasure in my work.

I tried to perform my job as if the forest I worked in was my own. What we do on it can affect others—man and beast. Clean air and clear water can and does happen all by itself. It's when we abuse what nature has given us that we muddy up the creek, foul our own nest.

The challenges of earning a living in the woods are many and substantial. As a one-man crew for any task that needed doing, I was the only volunteer. Amber-Jean was always there for moron support, and damn good at it. There were weeks on end where I was so busy you'd think I was a twin. If I wasn't logging, I was down at my dad's shop fixing something that broke or getting ready to break. He was a child of the Great Depression, and because of that, he never threw anything away that might be usable. He didn't call it recycling. He called it common sense. He'd look at something I broke and say, "I have just the thing to fix that. I've been saving it for thirty years." He'd go down in the bowels of the barn and come up with a part from an old baler, fix me up, and send me back to work. As I would leave, he'd smile and say, "Saved your ass again boy."

Or if I couldn't get the offending equipment to his shop, I'd be lying on the ground somewhere on a piece of cardboard under a truck, tractor, or bulldozer, in the rain or snow, freezing or frying. I'd be changing oil, greasing fittings, or replacing, pounding, and/or prying on something that needed it.

Now I had three chainsaws that needed tending to. Three were needed to keep two going. I'd learned it paid to use one chainsaw for cutting down trees in the woods, and I would strive to keep it razor sharp and cutting like a bandit. Another I would use on the landing for bucking logs and firewood once they were skidded out. This one's chain would take a beating because of the dirt that can be rubbed on the trees during the skidding process. The third I would keep in reserve and use where and when needed. It wasn't uncommon for me to have to file a chainsaw three or four times a day. I could file a chainsaw in about ten minutes, give or take. It depended on whether I was just touching it up or if I'd hit something serious and I needed to get it back up to snuff.

Blocking firewood into sixteen-inch lengths by hand with a chainsaw was taxing, backbreaking labor. It meant being bent over while running a chainsaw and rolling logs with a peavey. Sometimes I would have to use a hatchet and a wire brush to remove dirt and mud if the logs were coated heavily with it. Frozen mud was the worst. My skill with a file meant I was able to block up a full cord of wood in about an hour or so. It all depended on the diameter of the wood and how dirty it was. I would use two of my three chainsaws and tag-team the pile—use one saw until it was dull or out of gas, grab the other one, and keep blasting away until that one was played out. Or I was.

I'd have to stop blocking wood several times to chuck blocks out of my way so I could cut up stems that the blocks were lying on. The technique I found worked best was to cut two thirds of the way through each block of sixteen-inch firewood for the length of the log, then use the peavey to roll the log to expose the last third of the cut and finish it. This kept the saw chain from being pinched. It also allowed me to run the saw's chain in such a manner as to throw the muddy bark out of the cut instead of pulling it into the cut, and thereby extended the sharpness of the chain.

I'd end up with a long pile of sixteen-inch block wood all set for the wood splitter. Splitting wood with a wood splitter could be a real finger pounding affair if attention wasn't paid. Every blocked piece had to be picked up by hand and pushed through the splitting wedge with the hydraulic piston of the wood splitter. It's a piston that seems to move slower than God's wrath on a rain-soaked, bug-infested day. Sometimes, I'd sort through the easy splitting, straight-grained blocks and split them by hand with a splitting maul to make sure I was getting enough exercise. I'd set the gnarly chunks aside for the wood splitter. I'd throw the split wood in the truck for even more cardiovascular activity. It still took me about two hours to split and load a cord into the truck.

By the time I blocked the wood to sixteen-inches, split and threw it in the truck, and filed my chainsaws adequately, I was taking a good three hours or more to do a cord. I had to find a way to speed things up and remove the handling of each stick of firewood from of the equation. I felt like I was getting to know each piece of wood personally by the time I got it in the truck. I found the solution when I went to a logging equipment exposition. I watched a little thirty horse-power tractor run a Moelven log cleaver and I was sold.

The darn thing could block and split a cord of firewood in about half the time that I could with a wood splitter. And it was so simple. Hell, it only had two moving parts: a big honking hydraulic cylinder and a valve to control it. There's a PTO-driven hydraulic pump and a hydraulic oil tank, and the unit can be mounted to a tractor with a three-point hitch. It looked like a guillotine for wood. The unique design of the blade was the cat's granny. It used a sharp cutting blade with two wedges, one on each side of the blade. When it sheared through the log, it split it at the same time. It could shear up to thirteen-inch-diameter logs, so ninety-five percent of my firewood would go through it. Shoot, if the log was larger than that, I could usually get a saw log out of it. And dirty wood didn't bother it a bit.

I bought one for thirty-two hundred dollars and set it up so it would be stationary on the landing instead of using it on the three-point hitch. Then my dad went to work. He made a six-foot-long P.T.O. shaft to go from the cleaver to the tractor. I would back up to the cleaver, raise the log winch on my tractor, pull its short PTO shaft off the tractor's drive shaft, swing it to the side, and attach the cleaver's long shaft to it.

He made a fourteen-foot log deck that could hold a cord of wood and could be easily assembled and taken down for transportation. I used this to pile logs on to feed them into the cleaver. Then we bought some used forks, and Dad retrofitted them to the decking blade on my tractor's bucket loader so I could put them on and off in a jiffy with two pins. I would use them to fork up logs onto the deck. Then he made a sixteen-foot wood conveyor that caught the wood as it came off the cleaver and dropped it into the back of my truck. Was this man a mechanical genius or what? He was the best.

Now I could put a cord of wood in my truck in two hours or less. More importantly, I wasn't ready for the glue factory at the end of the day. I had a bit more step in my giddy up and my head didn't fall into my supper plate near so often.

The cleaver worked well but did have one drawback that I hadn't foreseen. It couldn't be used on frozen wood during the winter. The wood shattered into kindling-size sticks because the wood fibers were too brittle to be sheared when they were frozen. It sort of worked out, though, because I don't sell and deliver much firewood during the winter months anyway. People can't burn unseasoned, fresh-cut firewood. Access for delivery of wood into people's yards with snow on the ground made it prohibitive as well. After I got the cleaver, I made a concerted effort to have a winter job that consisted of logs. Often it was softwood that isn't used as firewood.

The cleaver did have one good attribute: when shearing the wood, it pushed a lot of moisture out the end of the block and out the other end of the log that it was being sheared from. I could catch a cup of water off of either end every time the blade sheared off a piece. Customers would tell me they loved my firewood because it dried quicker. Shearing also added a bit more kindling-sized pieces to the load, which came in handy to start fires in their stoves.

Chapter 28
Need a Tums?

It was the mid '90s when I started a job on Sherman Hollow Road in Hinesburg. I was harvesting hardwood saw logs, utilizing their tops for firewood, and removing low-quality firewood trees. There was no forester involved. After discussing the landowner's goals for the harvest, I was confident I could meet his objectives. I'd been cutting marked timber for years and felt I knew what could be sustainably harvested from a woodlot. And with my added knowledge gleaned from those same years working in the woods, I had a solid grasp of where equipment could go and where it should not.

My cousin, Alfalfa, lived about a mile away from the job on the family farm. He had helped me occasionally over the years and would be helping full time, since I was working close by. Al's a hard worker, but the guy never shuts up. I call him my "turd cousin." So much crap comes out of his mouth, I don't know whether to offer him a breath mint or a piece of toilet paper. I had the log cleaver set up and we were doing a stroke of business.

It was a Tuesday near the end of July. I remember this distinctly because people tend to remember when disaster strikes. I left at noon to deliver a cord of firewood. After making the delivery, I ate my lunch on the return trip. It was a peanut butter sandwich and a couple of Ring Dings. Health food. When I got back to the job, I started to get a bellyache. I sat, bent over, on a log, filing a chainsaw, and it went from bad to worse. The pain was so severe that I started to feel light-headed. Al was cutting some trees near the landing, but I couldn't get his attention, and I didn't think I could walk that far.

It was either lie down or fall down, so I crawled into the bed of the firewood truck, lying on the cool steel floor and sweating like the pig that knows he's dinner—A steady stream was running off the back of the truck. Salmon could've spawned up it. Al finally came up to see why I was lying in the truck, as it wasn't my customary noontime procedure.

"Whatcha laying in the truck for?"

"Somethings wrong. Can't move. Wicked stomach pain," I managed to gasp out.

"You want me get you a Tums?" the bonehead asked me.

"No. Get me an ambulance," I moaned.

"What? You funning me?"

"Ambulance. Now. Hurry."

Al jumped in his pickup truck and peeled out for his place. I passed out a couple times but came to when the Saint Michael's College Fire and Rescue Squad came screeching up. They hauled my ass out of the truck and into their ambulance and began asking me questions. They started looking me over, removing my shirt.

"What are you doing?" I asked.

"Looking for some sort of bug bite. Maybe you got bitten by a spider," one of the young paramedics replied.

"I didn't get bit by no spider. It's my gut. I got wicked pain in my stomach. I ate lunch and next thing I know I'm passing out with this stomach pain."

One of them was trying to start an IV while we were bouncing down the road and kept stabbing me and missing the vein. After the third try I told him he was done using me for a dart board.

"What did you have to eat?"

"A peanut butter sandwich and a couple of Ring Dings."

"Maybe he's got food poisoning."

"Wouldn't happen that fast," I moaned. I was quite confident I wasn't being done in by a Ring Ding gone rogue, but I felt like I was about to be done in by something.

We got to the ER and doctors checked me all over and asked me a dozen questions. They drew some blood and successfully started an IV, but still didn't have a clue as to what was causing my severe stomach pain. I was going into shock and starting to lose consciousness. They asked me who they should be calling, next-of-kin sort of thing, and I started to worry.

Karen and kids had gone to visit her brother on Cape Hatteras for a three-week vacation. They got down there just before a hurricane started working its way up the East Coast. Now Hurricane Bertha was blowing into the Cape. I gave the doctor my sister Betty's phone number. They got her on the horn and told her that her baby brother was in rough shape. Betty's been a nurse all her life, and a damn good one. She'd know what to do.

Hurricane Betty came blowing into the emergency room. I was lying there in agony, on the edge of consciousness, when my sister's sweet voice broke through my delirium. She was tearing the doctor a new one.

"What do you mean you don't know what's wrong with him?! Find out, damn it! And find out NOW!"

Way to go, Betty! God, I love my big sister!

It took the doctors another day to figure out I had acute pancreatitis. A gallstone was blocking my bile duct. I was in serious trouble. First, they had to try to keep other organs from shutting down. They did an endoscopy—sort of ran a plumber's snake down my gullet. They made a small incision next to the gallstone to try to get it to move and unblock the bile duct. The hope was they could avoid surgery if it was successful. It was not.

I was so weak they didn't dare to operate unless there was no other choice. They kept treating me with drugs, hoping it would get me strong enough for the operation. They had to shut down my digestive track. No food or water. They shoved a suction tube up my nose and into my stomach to keep it sucked dry. All I was allowed were a few ice chips. For a week.

The weather on Cape Hatteras finally cleared enough, and Karen took a puddle-jumper plane off that sand-blow her brother lives on and caught a flight home. She left the kids down there. No need in ruining their vacation just because hers was shot to hell. I'll never hear the end of this!

After a week of an ice-chip diet, the doctor told me they were ready to operate and remove my gallbladder. He explained how it was going to be a simple operation that would be done laparoscopically. He'll make two small incisions in my stomach—wouldn't even leave a scar. Just two little Band-Aids afterwards. He'd chop up and suck out my gallbladder. I came out of anesthesia, and it sucked all right. I had a massive bandage from below my bellybutton up to my nipples. I felt like I'd been slit crotch-to-eyeball with a dull deer antler.

The doctor said that when he got in there with the scope, he saw bile everywhere and he didn't like the look of it—had to pry me open and root around in there with a stick to see if he couldn't find that gosh darn gallbladder. Other than that, the operation was a piece of cake.

Running a chainsaw for years had given me wicked brutal abdominal muscles. Having my six-pack cut into two triplets and stapled back together took the wind right out of my sails. I felt like I'd been eaten by a wolf and shit over a cliff. It'd be a few weeks before I would be back to bulling speed.

I'd purchased some disability insurance a few years before and I was able to make a claim. It wasn't much money, but it was better than a tunk on the head with a pointy rock. Thank God Karen had health insurance on me through her employer. The hospital bill was over sixteen thousand dollars. I did lose twenty pounds and got down to a rawhide 155 pounds. All in all, I wouldn't recommend it as a weight-loss program. Just to be on the safe side, I haven't eaten another Ring Ding since.

Chapter 29
Size Does Matter

My philosophy had been to use equipment as small as possible, but still get the job done. My tractor and bulldozer had proven to be up to the task. But when the hydraulics on my tractor shit the bed, I started to have thoughts of acquiring a skidder. It was a major breakdown. It required the tractor to be split in half to fix it. The strain that the winch was putting on the hydraulic system to lift the logs off the ground for skidding was taking its toll.

The size of the hitch I could skid was limited as well: maybe half a cord on average. The bulldozer could pull a larger hitch, but it wasn't wise to skid a long distance with it. The tracks of a bulldozer are all steel on steel. They wear out and are a hell of a lot more expensive than tires. What's called the undercarriage (the large drive sprockets and big front idler wheels, the top and bottom rollers, plus the chain and the grouser pads of the track) adds up to big bucks to replace.

I knew from the beginning that my equipment was restricting the jobs I could work by not being able to profitably skid timber long distances. Skidding beyond five hundred yards was too far to skid without losing my shirt financially and wearing the snot out of my equipment, to boot. I had always accepted this and worked around it. But lately I had turned down some nice jobs because of these limitations.

A skidder would change the size of the hitch I could pull and the distance I could skid it economically. One thing it wouldn't change was my ability and determination to do quality work. I vowed to keep the skidder on the main skid road and bunch trees to it with my 450C. The ability of the bulldozer to turn on a dime and give you nine cents change cannot be overstated. This maneuverability while bunching stems, along with the use of the blade to directionally push trees over, made a difference in the quality of the work—little, subtle advantages that make a lasting difference to the forest but almost go unnoticed to the untrained eye. It's a quality that skidding trees from the stump with a skidder just can't match.

Being able to use the bulldozer to repair old log roads and put in new ones, as well as put the roads to bed with water bars and broad-based dips was huge. Roads are forever, or should be considered so when deciding when and where to build one. Landowners loved knowing their roads would be constructed correctly and be in good shape for years to come. It was a component of my work they were willing to pay for, too, either outright by an hourly rate or with reduced stumpage for their timber. A skilled worker can't perform work for free. I believe if a person wants something done good, fast, and cheap: pick two. Because that's all you're going to get, especially when it comes to logging.

I decided I would sell the tractor. And without the tractor to run it, I would sell the log cleaver and conveyor and get out of selling and delivering firewood. Hundreds of cords had gone through the cleaver during the last five years and I'd enjoyed not having to deal with firewood customers during the time I worked with Charlie. My love of making a difference on the land was winning out over the time spent processing and delivering firewood. Having to answer the phone day and night to take orders was a drag too. Scheduling delivery, coordinating where customers wanted it dumped, and getting payment was a boil on the backside as well.

"So, I'll be there between four and four thirty with your cord of firewood. Where would you like me to dump it?"

"Could you dump it inside the garage?"

"No. The dump box on my truck doesn't allow that. It raises up about twelve feet when it dumps the wood out."

"Well that's very inconvenient."

Or the time I delivered a load of wood with a lot of red oak in it, which is high quality firewood and has its own earthy fragrance.

"Eew! The wood smells funny. Are you sure it's okay?"

"Yes. Its red oak. Great firewood. That's what it smells like."

"Is it going to smell like that when I burn it?"

"Let's hope so."

The firewood truck could hit the road too. I'd sell my firewood in log length to a firewood processor. I went shopping for a skidder. Charlie's Timberjack skidder performed admirably and under adverse conditions. Timberjack skidders are stable, solid working machines, especially the older ones that I could afford. I found a good used 230 Timberjack in my price range at Pete's Repair in Morrisville, but it didn't have an apron. Pete showed me a tiny little apron he had, and I turned up my nose at it. I spied one off to the side of his yard. It was a nice wide one off a Clark Ranger that afforded good protection to the tires and axles. I told him that if he would mount that sucker on the Jack, we would have us a deal. I was soon the proud owner of a cross-bred skidder—a Timber-Ranger, or a Ranger-Jack, whatever name snaps your garter. I sold my tractor, wood shearer, and firewood truck to get the money for the purchase.

Chapter 30
A Rabble Alliance:
May the Forest Be With You

I was only one man, and my experience and skill with a chainsaw and equipment were best spent cutting and landing timber. If I wanted my work to count for something—make the forest a better place—I needed to concentrate my time, expertise, and aptitude where it could do the most good. My observations had shown me that some folks needed to be enlightened as to what working in the woods in the right way meant to the forest and society. I would sometimes be in social situations where a person would ask what I did for a living.

"So, what do you do for work?"

"I'm a timber-harvesting technician."

It'd usually take a few seconds, then it would slowly sink in. "Oh, a logger. Where do you work?"

"In the woods."

There were instances when a person found out I was a logger, and I could feel their air of disapproval. Like a wet dog at a wedding. They would rarely have the courage to discuss their concerns with me. I suppose it's the same reason that people are more opposed to fur than leather—it's a lot easier to pick on women than bikers.

Occasionally, when they would say how wrong it was to cut trees, I would smile and politely ask them what their house was made of. Did they know the source of the wood in their house and the furniture in it? Was it local wood or imported? Sustainably harvested or from some butcher job? And, by God, it better not be from a rainforest! I would point out numerous wood products around us. The chair they had their ass parked on, the table they were eating off of, the floor they were standing on. They would point out that they recycle, some even using recycled toilet paper. Frankly, I think that's going a bit too far. If somebody's already wiped their ass with it, I don't want to use it again.

I was deeply engrossed in my work and content doing the best I could in my local forests and keeping a low profile. Some people who frown on cutting trees would state they were conservationists. They recycled, composted, belonged to the Sierra Club. I was the real deal conservationist. I'd take care of the forest one acre at a time every day on the job. I would let my work do my talking for me. But there was one person who felt the need to speak out, to educate and instruct the landowners and the public that there are better, healthier ways to go into our forests for the wood products we need: my forester friend David Brynn.

David had been the Addison County Forester for years now. He had walked their lands, observed their forest management practices, listened to their plans and goals for their forests. He saw numerous obstacles preventing them from achieving those goals. He saw that many forest landowners lacked the knowledge and support necessary to apply forestry practices that would be beneficial for them and the whole forest community. He realized that, too often, it was competition and the bottom-line driving forest management, the result being timber harvests that were rough on the woods, and most of the money going to the mills or log buyers.

This situation led to David's founding Vermont Family Forests (www.familyforests.org). It would fill in those gaps of information and supply the support that conscientious landowners were craving. It would be an organization whose aim, first and foremost, was to put the health of the forest front and center. And then, if fitting, to foster careful cultivation of those forests for community benefits, such as firewood, saw logs, and maple syrup.

It's Wendell Berry's contention that the two great ruiners of private land are ignorance and economic constraint. And Aldo Leopold's perception is that the absence of a land ethic perpetuates land abuse. The truths of these two conservationists led David to the idea that the three conservers of family forests are informed landowners, sound economic returns for ecological forestry, and a community-shared land ethic. He cut through the rind and got down to the melon.

In 1996, VFF identified 32 forest landowners of about five thousand acres having an excellent track record of sound stewardship, and they formed a pool of well-managed, family-owned forests. These VFF members' lands became certified through the Forest Stewardship Council (FSC) and VFF was up and running.

David contacted me and asked if I wanted to be involved as the logger that would carry out the work for harvesting projects on VFF member's woodlots. I would be harvesting FSC-certified timber to provide wood for local building projects—wood that is grown and harvested in ways that are restorative, sustainable, efficient, local and fair.

I'm smart enough to eat the fruit of opportunity when it falls off the tree. We began a collaborative relationship that turned out better than I hoped and lasted for many years. It was the basis for some of the best forestry I ever had the privilege of doing during my career in the woods. Over the years, I would supply sustainably harvested, third party–certified timber for building projects at Middlebury College, Shelburne Museum, the Green Mountain Club, the University of Vermont, and the Lake Champlain Maritime Museum, to name a few. I can go to the Maritime Museum and get in a boat made from a white pine I'd carefully harvested from a woodlot just six miles away. I'll bet you a cookie there aren't a lot of loggers who can do that!

The neat thing about VFF was they had an inventory of the wood on their members' property. They worked as the liaison between their members and clients who wanted to build using sustainably harvested local wood. When the Green Mountain Club needed twenty-four-foot hemlock beams for its new headquarters, VFF looked in its members' inventory and found who had hemlock of the size needed, with willing land owners ready to harvest it. Then VFF worked out the details for me to go and get it.

It was a radical concept compared to the way wood is traditionally procured from the land. We wouldn't cut the whole woodlot. Instead, we would just take what the forest was ready to give to meet our needs. Similar to going in the garden and picking what's ripe. Hell, you don't have to dynamite the whole dang pond to get the fish you want. It worked out better for the landowner, the client buying the lumber, and the logger cutting the trees. But more importantly, it was a better deal for the forest.

I worked on some fine woodlots for Vermont Family Forests. One of the best was when I worked on Middlebury College's property to supply timber for McCardell Bicentennial Hall, a $40 million, 220,000-square-foot science building. Middlebury College has thousands of acres of forest land that surround its Bread Loaf Campus in Ripton, yet this would be the first time the college used its own timber to build on campus in a hundred years. Go figure.

Part of the arrangement with Middlebury College was that its lands forester, Steve Webber, would be helping me on the job as the cutter. I've always shied away from having people work with me. It can be more dangerous to work with an inexperienced person than it is to work alone. But it didn't take me long to realize I had nothing to worry about with Steve. The man had woods savvy. The guy was in his sixties and could out-work me any day of the week. He'd worked in the woods from Maine to Alaska. And like me, he let his work speak for itself.

I also had another new partner on the job. Amber-Jean Marie, the most steadfast and faithful log-dog I'd ever known, had gone to her reward a couple years past. Through fifteen years of service and devotion to my family, she had showed us what unconditional love was all about. And though she could never be replaced in my heart, her replacement in the woods was coming on strong and doing an admirable job. Jacob was a long-legged, deep-chested black Lab and took to the woods with an intelligence I'd rarely seen in a dog.

One glorious October morning when Steve and I were working together up on Bread Loaf, I came back into the woods to get a hitch with the skidder. Jacob would lead the way in and out of the woods, scouting along about twenty yards ahead of me. The woods were just alive with color, with the road sprinkled with freshly falling leaves and a coolness in the air that made working in the woods a pure pleasure. Fall is my favorite time of year and I'd savor the days like this one I was blessed with. No time clocks to punch. No boss looking over my shoulder. I loved the freedom my work gave me.

I shut off the skidder, climbed out of it, and looked over to where my bulldozer sat, about fifty yards to my right. Lo and behold, there was the biggest darn bull moose I'd ever laid eyes on, standing within a few feet of the dozer, his shoulder well above its hood. His massive antlers spread about five feet; his breath puffed out in steamy, white billows through the cool fall air. In the bright fall sunlight, the vibrant colors of the woods contrasted with his nearly black body. Jake saw him, too, and started a deep growl in his chest as the hair rose up on his shoulders and down his spine.

"Sit boy!" I said, and his ass hit the dirt.

"Good boy. Stay!" I walked up and clipped a leash on him. I always kept one handy for reasons such as this and I was happier than hell that I had it with me now.

Steve, who had just finished cutting a hitch, was seventy-five yards off to my left and I gave a shout. He came walking up and I pointed out the bull.

"Holy moley! Would you look at the size of that moose! He's just about the biggest bull I've ever seen, and I've seen a lot of moose in my day," Steve said as we stood gawking at the massive creature. "I bet that ol' boy will top a thousand pounds."

"Would you go over there and shoo him away from my dozer so I can bunch the next hitch?"

"Nope! He's in rut. Look at him. He's been wallowing. And he's not scared of us one bit. A lot of people have been stomped by a moose."

I handed him Jake's leash and walked half the distance toward the moose, and he stood there eyeballing me like money from home.

"Go on! Get out of here!" I shouted and clapped my hands. He didn't budge. He pawed a big clump of the forest floor with his front hoof and threw it about twenty feet into the air behind him.

"I'd leave him alone. You don't want to get him riled," Steve warned me.

I walked back to the skidder and we stood there and watched him for a few minutes. Godfrey, but he was magnificent! I had an idea.

"Hell, we got to bunch those trees. I ain't paid by the hour," I said as I climbed up on the skidder and grabbed my chainsaw.

"I'm going to start this sucker up and walk toward him with it running. I bet he won't like the sound of it." I flipped the kill-switch to "run" and set the choke. Another thought came to me as I grasped the starter cord.

"If he don't run off and I get in trouble, let Jake loose."

That big bluffer couldn't take it, and when I got to within about thirty feet of him, revving up the chainsaw, he turned and ran. When he got about forty yards away, he stopped, turned around and looked at me with a real disgusted look, like I hadn't played fair, and he might just come back and give me a go. But he turned and trotted off, disappearing into the autumn understory like a puff of his breath.

A bit later, I was unhooking my chokers from the trees I'd just bunched when a Middlebury College professor with a group of students came walking up the road. They all had on backpacks and most had notepads out. We talked about the woods and why I was cutting the trees as Jake sniffed them out and made friends.

"Have you seen any wildlife while you've been working here?" he asked. "We saw some fresh moose tracks down the road."

"If you'd been here a while ago, you'd have seen their maker. It was one heck of a big bull," I informed him.

"Really? Which way did he go? The students would love to see him."

I pointed in the direction the old warrior had retreated.

"He wandered off that way, but if I were you, I'd give him a wide berth. He ain't in no mood for company unless you're a female moose. I had to persuade him to leave, and if you hunt him up, you just might see more of him than you'd care to."

He looked at me like he thought I was yanking his chain, then they all wandered off in the direction the moose had gone. I figured if they caught up with that cantankerous old boy, they might get some firsthand instruction on love-sick moose behavior. They could jot it down in their notepads on the run.

Now that I was a seasoned veteran of the woods, one might think I would be working through the days unscathed by the dangers lurking in the great outdoors where I earned my living. The fact is, I was having close calls on a regular basis. I still had bruises and scratches show up in the shower and couldn't recall how they got there. I'd become immune to the recognition of getting banged up and knocked around and had subconsciously accepted it as a standard practice of wielding a chainsaw and running equipment.

About every month or two, I had a near miss. If I wasn't in tune to my surroundings, if I hadn't developed a sixth sense as to what might happen, I would've been hurt or possibly killed.

I was getting older, and maybe a step slower, but my knowledge was greater, my instincts were to be trusted. When about to do something and my Spidey sense started tingling, I'd stop and assess the situation; maybe alter how I was going to do it. If I had a gut feeling to look up, it was immediately obeyed, the falling branch seen, the danger avoided. I got to cut another tree; pull another hitch; work another day.

I secured a large job in Hanksville for a maple syrup maker with eleven thousand taps. He'd bought some additional acreage and wanted to thin out trees that weren't sugar maples before he ran his pipeline through the woods. It was a long, downhill skid, almost a mile to the back boundary. I was grateful I now had a skidder that could handle the job.

The day was going well as I began the afternoon stretch. I was on rough ground as I drove into an area with the bulldozer where I was cutting my third hitch of the day. I left her idling while I took a few minutes to scope things out. As I climbed off the left side of the bulldozer, a strap on my safety chaps looped over the forward-reverse lever, shifting her into reverse, and I lost my balance as I was stepping onto the track. She took off! I grabbed onto a handle on top of the battery box as I drove my knees onto the moving steel track. As an added bonus, I pounded my head into the pipe that's part of the canopy. Luckily, my hard hat took the brunt of the blow, and it went flying off. I was left hanging by that goddamn strap on the side of the dozer going backwards!

I tried to get my feet back under me, but it was like being strapped on a treadmill going sideways and I kept stumbling and falling down. Did it three or four times. I almost started to laugh as I pictured what this must look like. Then I glanced in the direction I was going, and all humor evaporated. There was a ledge with an eight-foot drop only twenty yards away, and I was headed right for it! This had an accelerated effect on my activity. I heaved myself up off the track using the handle, the canopy-support pipe, and sheer upper-body strength that a massive shot of adrenalin has been known to produce.

I was really moving along now. "Getting off the track won't save me or the bulldozer," I thought. "I've got to get in the seat and put my foot on the brake. Right now!" I lunged for the seat. Because of the strap, I had to turn my ass into it. (Picture a video clip run in reverse of how I got into this freaking mess. Now run it at double speed.) This took the twist out of the strap, and I slipped it off the lever in a frantic, lucky maneuver as I flopped into the seat. I overshot it and drove the winch control lever on the other side of the seat into my right thigh. Yowzer! I threw the forward-reverser into neutral with my left hand, ignored the stabbing pain in my thigh, jammed my right foot down on the brake, and jerked to a stop.

I turned and looked behind me. I was about five feet short of pitching over the ledge. Another second or two … I pulled the dozer ahead as I turned it parallel to the run of the ledge, put the blade down, applied down-pressure, and shut her off. I was still shaking as I massaged the bruise in my thigh. I knew I'd have a charley horse that could run a steeple chase. It turned all sorts of cool colors. I'd also have no trouble remembering where I got this one. I worked my way out of it.

Chapter 31
Forward Into the Woods

I believed that, in the right hands, a 230 Timberjack and a John Deere 450C made one of the best combinations to yard timber in an efficient and ecologically healthy manner. Still do. But I came to realize it didn't hold true in every situation. There's terrain in Vermont where only a skidder can go because of the steep hills. And there are some real nasty spots where only a bulldozer can creep into. But skidding's a real drag. Always landing wood by dragging it on the ground has consequences that need to be acknowledged.

Soil disturbance caused by the weight of the logs gouging along behind the skidder can be excessive, and ruts are dug by tires with chains required to pull all that dragged weight. When it's skidded up, down, and over hills and through wet spots, erosion is unavoidable. Sometime, when the skidder can't pull a hitch through a mud hole, the winch is released and the hitch dropped so the skidder can get through it. Then the logs get winched through the mud hole and up to the skidder apron. This scrapes out the mudhole and makes it worse.

Cutting up mud-encrusted logs and firewood really bites the big one. It dulls a chainsaw pretty damn quick. Then there's the need to jockey around and push up logs with the skidder on the landing. It's not like a car or tractor where the front wheels turn to steer it. A skidder hinges in the middle and is hydraulically angled to make turns. It almost always has tire chains on it. This causes it to tear up the ground on the landing something fierce, especially if the landing gets muddy from rain. Some landowners don't want to have a skidder on their property. Others look at them as a necessary evil—like having to pick a presidential candidate to vote for.

David Brynn brought up the idea of using a forwarder to forward wood from the forest instead of skidding it. Scandinavian countries had been doing it for a while. A forwarder is a wheeled vehicle that carries logs from the woods to the landing with the logs stacked in a bunk. It carries logs off the ground and impacts the soil less but has a limit on the length of the logs it can move. It has a boom-type log loader, or cherry picker, similar to those used on a log truck.

I started researching forwarders to see if one might suit me for the work I was doing. I found that full-size, self-powered models cost more than Alaska, as well as being only slightly smaller. But I did discover companies that were manufacturing forwarding trailers. These could be towed behind a four-wheel-drive tractor and were much more affordable. With my history of running a tractor, the idea caught my fancy.

I talked to Art about what I was thinking. I was always bouncing stuff off him and telling him my troubles. We'd talk about a near miss I had or the latest battles with the weather and busted equipment. Discuss how our kids were doing. Plan an evening out with our wives. Go hunting or fishing. He'd tell me of his latest skirmish concerning his Crohn's disease. Even if he was losing a round or two, he never bitched. He always offered me a willing ear, sound advice, and an encouraging word. I tried to do the same. We went through the pros and cons of switching to a forwarder.

A forwarding wagon towed by a tractor can't go up and down steep hills or wander off the main wood's road. It's not maneuverable enough nor protected underneath. Having to load light and go often when pulling uphill would be bothersome. But the same can be said for a skidder. Taking a loaded forwarder wagon downhill, discovering the tractor's brakes can't hold it back, and piling up in a twisted wreck would be annoying as hell too. There weren't brakes on the trailers. The tractor's brakes would be the only brakes. I'd have to keep it on good roads and bunch wood to it. On rough, nasty, steep terrain, I may have to bunch farther with the dozer. Not a big deal, especially if I chose my jobs wisely. Maybe Dad could rig up a drag chute.

Moving it from one job site to another had its pluses and minuses. I could drive the tractor and forwarder wagon down the town roads with a "Slow Moving Vehicle" sign on it. To move the skidder I had to hire a trucker at the cost of sixty bucks an hour, but I'd have to remove the tractor's tire chains to haul the forwarder wagon down the town roads. Having to wrestle them back on when I got to the next job would be just like work. I figured I could tell myself I was making sixty dollars per hour.

A forwarder wagon would keep my logs cleaner. I would be bunching stems to staging areas along the main forwarding road, and they wouldn't pick up much dirt during the short skid. I'd cut them into log lengths and load them onto the forwarder wagon in the woods, which would allow me to sort out any rotten wood and eliminate other material I was skidding for no value. These usually end up an eyesore on the landing and a headache to deal with. Instead, I could leave them in the forest where they could go back into the soil.

If I had a forwarder, I could use the cherry picker to separate firewood from logs as I loaded the trailer, loading one or the other first. Then on the landing, I could pull up to the appropriate pile and unload. I could even sort logs for different markets and load trucks with it. It would enable me to have smaller and neater landings because of the ability to stack piles of logs taller, thereby needing less space. On small woodlots with limited landing areas, this would be beneficial. I was starting to see many reasons to switch to a forwarder.

I've heard change is the one constant in life. It's been stated, "The way up and the way down are one and the same." I was forty-eight now and knew I still had a stretch of logging ahead of me. I'd been working in the woods for over thirty years. Being in the forest, and the living I'd scratched from it, had been more fun than spitting off a bridge. I hadn't gotten rich, but I'd had a rich life. Cripes, if money talks, mine's always said "goodbye." I sold the skidder and put the proceeds toward a Hardy 1700 ST forwarding trailer and a Duetz-Fahr sixty horsepower four-wheel-drive tractor.

The tractor was a sweet one I found in Concord, Vermont. A dealership out in the Midwest had sold out and the unit ended up there. It only had ninety hours on it and was just what I was looking for. A Duetz-Fahr is a European-made tractor with brakes on both the front and rear wheels. Most all American-made tractors only have rear brakes. I figured I'd need all the braking power I could get to hold back a loaded trailer of wood going down hills. This proved to be true.

I bought the Hardy from the same dealer that sold me the tractor. We did some dickering and I got it forty-five hundred dollars cheaper than from other sources. It could reach out seventeen feet with the boom on the cherry picker and lift over a thousand pounds out there. At four feet away, it could lift over three thousand pounds. It could carry close to two cord of wood or damn near a thousand board feet of saw logs in the twelve-foot log bunk. This was comparable to what my skidder could pull on an average hitch.

I took the tractor down to Dad's shop to get it ready for the woods. With Dad and Art's help, we built a steel canopy over the operator, with limb risers from the top of it to the nose of the tractor. Then we made an ingenious box-type hitch that would allow the draw-bar to pivot up and down as well as swing side to side at the hitch pin. This design was needed when going through water bars and broad-based dips. The trailer came standard with a rotating hitch on the tow tongue so if the trailer flipped over, it wouldn't flip the tractor too. Thank God it was there: I had it about an hour before I flipped her over.

I'd brought it home to learn how to run it and figured loading a few big brush piles down back would be a good place to start. I pulled up to a pile and set my stabilizer legs down on either side, swung the boom over, and commenced loading. I'd run excavators before to put in roads for landowners, and the controls are quite similar. With that fifty-inch wide grapple, I soon had the pile loaded and pulled ahead to the next one. I was happier than a cat at a fish fry.

I hopped up on the loader, swung the boom over to grab more brush, and over she went. I'd forgot to put my stabilizer legs down. I was fortunate to be doing things slow, just learning, and immediately dropped the boom to the ground, almost keeping it from going over.

I didn't have any equipment handy to stand her back up—my bulldozer was waiting on a job. But since I'm still smarter than your average bear, I was able to manipulate the boom in conjunction with the stabilizer leg and got her righted. The next day I bought some stick-on lettering. On the A-frame of the loader, right in front of where the operator stands, eyeball level, in big, bold lettering, I wrote: PUT LEGS DOWN! And I never flopped her over again.

Art did.

He forgot to put the stabilizer legs down the first day he ran it helping me at the Little Hogback Community Forest in Monkton. It wasn't long after he headed out with his first wagonload that he came walking back up from the landing, looking pretty sheepish. I knew exactly what he'd done. He was next to the log pile, which stopped her from going all the way over. With the weight from the load of red oak saw logs in the bunk, I thought it was best to get the bulldozer and gently pull her over as Art helped run the boom and stabilizer legs. Nothing got hurt but Art's pride.

These types of mishaps were constant reminders of how logging can be a game of inches. One simple mistake when a lever isn't pushed down for a few seconds to lower a stabilizer and things go sideways. Nobody's perfect. Hell, even monkeys fall out of trees now and then.

*   *   *

Jacob and I are were tight as man and dog can be. A guy's never lonely if he's got his dog. But in the last few years, I'd become aware of ticks in the woods, and they bite man and dog. I pulled a couple off me, so I began doing tick checks on Jake and found more on him. I'd never had to worry about ticks in all my years in the woods. Now I had to do tick checks on Jake and me every day. Climate change is real and the effects are many. The diseases ticks transmit are of grave concern. My daughter and my grandson have both tested positive for Lyme disease.

One evening, Jake wouldn't eat his food. Nor the next day. I took him to my vet, who did some blood work. My boy had Lyme disease. His kidneys were failing and there wasn't a damn thing that I could do. I spent the next day with him, doing all I could to keep him comfortable, keep him close, and try to return some of the love he'd given me over the last eight years. I realized I was doing it for my sake, not his, and that I had to let go. I asked the vet to come to the house. I held Jacob in my arms and watched the life go out of his eyes as tears welled up in mine.

The days seemed mighty lonely for a while, but I've discovered one of the best ways to get through grief is to work hard at something worth doing, and I found comfort in the woods. I always have. A person who takes a good, long look at nature can come to grips with life's challenges a lot easier. It helps in understanding that losses are part of the game. Strikes and gutters. I've learned to be grateful for the good that we do have in life, and when that rough spot in the road needs to be traveled, to know that this, too, will pass.

It would be a few months, but I couldn't deny the fact that I needed a dog. I've never been without one for long. I purchased a yellow Lab in memory of Amber-Jean Marie and named him Levi; it was my dad's middle name. He ain't the sharpest nail in the keg, but he'll do. Starting out training him was a chore. It reminded me of teaching my turd cousin Alfalfa to log. Every Monday morning it felt like I was starting from scratch. Levi's learning capacity could be better, but he tries, and that's what counts.

Chapter 32
Rolling Along

Logging is a disturbance. One could say it's a natural disturbance, but that's crazy talk. Crazy that I am, I could argue that if you believe man is part of nature, by extension, man's harvesting and removal of wood from a forest is part of nature too. It's been going on for quite a spell. But there's a sight of difference between what man took from the forest over the centuries and what man has been removing from the forest during the last hundred years. And I wouldn't say our track record is so stellar that we should be patting each other on the back.

At this point in my journey, I felt certain I owned some of the best type of logging equipment available. It allowed me to harvest timber with a light footprint on the land, when used with care and patience. I couldn't log wicked steep, mountain goat terrain, but I didn't want to. I'd had my fill of that. I also believe there are places that should be left alone. I'd taken Dirty Harry's words to heart about how a man's got to know his limitations. And thankfully, I've come to know mine.

I realized it when David Brynn showed me a woodlot he thought might be of interest. When we cruised the land, it didn't take me long to grasp that, although it had some decent timber on it, this wasn't a place for my tractor and forwarder wagon. I declined the job. I recommended he get somebody with a skidder, which he did. The poor bastard rolled the skidder and got staved up. Damn near killed. If not for my capacity to admit the boundaries of my abilities, I may well have been the one lying in the cold mud, pinned under equipment, alone on a mountainside.

I'll readily point out that I'm not perfect. I guess I'm a procrastinating perfectionist: maybe someday I'll be perfect. It's impossible to always get things right when it comes to working in the woods. Or life. But *trying* to get things right, that is something I could achieve. And I think it's that trait that's got me the chance to work in a way that's done more than just satisfy my wallet. It satisfied my soul. It verified the reasons, the very essence of why I went into the woods every morning.

I've harvested timber for boats that kids built at the Lake Champlain Maritime Museum. I've cut the trees for a replica of a 17th century post-and-beam barn for Shelburne Museum and helped raise it. I can walk through the Green Mountain Club's headquarters and see and touch the hemlock beams, knowing that it was my skill and knowledge with saw and equipment that carefully laid the hemlock down and enabled it to serve and shelter us in a splendid, worthy way.

As my logging career progressed, so did the machinery that evolved in the wood-harvesting industry. My opinion, based on my observations and experience, is that the driving force for equipment research and development is to cut more trees faster and safer. To get them off the stump and onto a truck, be it logs or chips, with the minimal amount of manual labor. Do it as quickly as possible and in a way that landowners and foresters will still tolerate the methods and machinery. Time is money. Having it all be profitable is at the top of the list. And if there's enough money to be had, the means will justify the end. I've said it before: if a forest landowner wants things done good, fast, and cheap, pick two, because that's all you're going to get.

Who was I to say that sitting in a heated/air-conditioned cab of a mechanical harvesting, tree-snipping machine is any better or worse than the way I was getting logs to the landing? Is just being easier and faster better? Could be. What defines "better or worse"? Workers' compensation insurance rates for an operator in the cab of a mechanical tree harvester are a hell of a lot better than they are for a logger on the ground running a chainsaw. But like many things, one size doesn't fit all, and that goes for mechanical harvesting too.

I've yet to see a woodlot lightly harvested by this type of equipment. This is because it can't do it economically. Some will argue what "lightly harvested" means. Just because the forest can take it doesn't mean it's healthy for it. The overhead cost of mechanical harvesting is so high it can't travel through a woodlot cutting a tree here and there. Nor can it do the small, fragmented woodlots that are being created. I bet the owner of a mechanical harvester knows how many trees have to be within its grasp every hour to make it pay. And so do the foresters working with them, and they treat the woodlot accordingly.

What has to be cut to make it economically viable may not be what the landowner wants ... or the forest. But what choice does the landowner have when the logger using a chainsaw is going the way of the cowboy? There's very little training for entry-level chainsaw loggers. Even some of the operators running mechanical harvesters are getting injured, because on the few occasions when they have to get out of the cab and run a chainsaw, they're too out of shape and untrained to do so.

And the new dangers of running mechanized logging equipment haven't been fully addressed. The falling tree isn't killing them. It's moving large volumes on landings with large equipment like log loaders, chippers, delimbers and slasher saws and working to repair them. As for the youths of today heading into the woods to work, they aren't. It's real work that many have no taste for. Few parents want their children to work in the deadliest profession in the nation. Mine didn't.

The fact is, small-volume operators of my type aren't ever going to meet the the market-driven demands that mankind is placing on the forest. How these demands are met while still protecting other values and benefits that are held in a healthy forest—ones that don't come in the shape of wood on a truck—is a pursuit that needs the utmost consideration. I've watched for years as the wood products industry bulled its way through the forest in search of that answer. My own remedy was to take my tiny equipment and my faithful dog and gently work my way among the trees, pausing only briefly to tilt at an occasional windmill.

Throughout the years I toiled in the woods, I became more aware of my place in it. Some would say I was just a logger. That all I did was cut down trees. The tasks that I performed to get a log roadside went far beyond the mere cutting down of a tree. I had no crew. Work that needed to be done, I did it. I cruised the land and the timber; fixed up old roads and log landings; laid out and built new roads and landings. I was an equipment mechanic, chainsaw mechanic, saw filer, log scaler, log marketer. I was the cutter, the buncher, log bucker, forwarder operator or skidder driver, grease monkey, and fuel man. If I didn't do it, it didn't get done.

When things broke, I fixed them. Or if beyond my ability, I got them fixed somehow. My dad's workshop was usually the first destination on the journey to repair something that was broken. But that pillar of strength I could always count on is gone. Alzheimer's disease took my dad. Every 65 seconds, someone in the United States develops Alzheimer's (Alzheimer's Association). I'd witnessed the man who could remember fifty things a day, while running a fleet of buses, not remember what he had for breakfast.

It wasn't long after I'd lost Jake that I started to see signs in Dad that were more than simple forgetfulness. His shop, usually neat as a pin, would be cluttered with tools and projects unfinished. He couldn't remember where the tools went. Couldn't stay on task. And he knew it was happening. He told me he'd rather lose a leg than his mind. Said he could get a wooden leg; couldn't get a wooden brain. He didn't want to end up like his dad, slumped in a wheelchair in a nursing home, drooling on himself. I promised him I'd do all I could to keep him in his home—the house he'd built from the ground up in a cow pasture; built with his own two hands and raised six kids in.

When the end came, it was quick and merciful. Dad went in the hospital for removal of a kidney stone. A day or two after the procedure, I guess something just gave out. I couldn't bear an autopsy, so whether it was his heart or an aneurism, I'll never know. What I did know was that his suffering had ended, and on his terms. He still knew he was home and that he was loved.

My family's roots in the hills of Vermont go long and deep. My father made sure I knew them and understood why. When my great-great-great-grandfather Samuel picked up a rifle and joined eighty-two other Green Mountain Boys to capture Fort Ticonderoga in 1775, he began a tradition in my family: one that states that we stand up and do what we can for our fellow man and the place we call home; one my dad continued when he enlisted in the Navy after Pearl Harbor. He may have been just a Vermont country lad who had never left his home state, but he knew he had to try to make a difference and lend a hand.

When shipped to Missouri for diesel school, he graduated first in his class of 250 and was thus allowed to choose where to serve. The Submarine Corps is for volunteers only, and the physical and psychological tests to enter are daunting. He fought in the South Pacific on the *USS Thresher*, the most decorated sub of World War II. I took the strength of his courage with me into the woods every day. The work ethic that drove me to excel at what I do, I learned from my dad.

Robert Frost summed up everything he learned about life in three simple words: "It goes on." Once again, I threw myself into my work, and with Levi's company, I figured out how to do things better with the forwarder. Bunching trees with the bulldozer for the forwarder required a different mindset than when bunching trees for a skidder. Stems needed to be brought to an area where the road was flat. The log loader couldn't swing logs uphill nor stop them from swinging downhill. Positioning bunched stems parallel to the forwarder road worked better than perpendicular. I used the log loader to lift and hold a stem while it was cut into proper lengths for the mill and to fit on the wagon. This made for easier bucking because I wouldn't be bent over or unknowingly cut into the ground or a stone.

The loader on the wagon soon became like a mechanical extension of my hand. I could reach out and grab a log without even thinking about what levers I had to manipulate. I wondered if that's how an operator of a mechanical harvester experiences the woods. Is it the only connection to the tree he has? Does he only see the forest through the glass of his cab?

When I was felling trees with a chainsaw, I walked up to a tree to be cut and put my hands on it, often hugging it, as I asked it questions. What's the best way to fall you to get you out of the woods? Which way are you leaning? What neighboring trees need to be guarded from harm as I take you from your place in the forest? How healthy are you? What value do you have? What defects can I see? And is there anything I can see in you, on you, or around you that's a hazard to me when I lay you down?

I imagine there are some things gained by being safe inside a cab to cut down a tree. I also wonder if there might be some things lost as well.

Chapter 33
Kneeded In the Worst Way

Years into forwarding timber, I found myself on a job near Sugarbush ski area. The woodlot access had a lot to be desired. Thankfully, David Brynn convinced the landowner of the value of good roads and he agreed to foot the bill for road construction. I rented an excavator for a week, and using it and my bulldozer, I constructed a nice road at a decent grade. I began to work the woodlot. The trees marked to cut were a mix of hardwood logs with a lot of firewood.

The work went along merry as a wedding bell, and as August approached I was winding-up the job. On a Monday morning I took a quick walk of what was left to cut and decided to call Jerry, my log and equipment trucker. Jerry had purchased Charlie Grant's log truck and was working on his own now—and still a wild man, as required by his occupation. We agreed to move my bulldozer on Saturday to my next job in Stowe. I'd signed a contract with Trapp Family Lodge to cut eighty cords of log-length firewood for their condos and time-share properties.

Thursday arrived, and I had about a dozen trees left to cut. It was a beautiful day, and around nine o'clock, I was working on the downhill side of my forwarder road, bunching trees with the dozer. I walked up to my next tree to cut. It was a white ash with a thirty-inch DBH and a massive crown. I was able to roll it down into a small opening I'd prepared by dropping and lopping up two small beech trees.

I worked along the right-hand side of the ash, cutting off limbs flush to the main stem, real slow and careful. The tree rolled its way to the ground, and in doing so, put a ton of tension on the branches due to the twisting as the tree came to rest. The main stem of the ash was held about three feet off the ground by all the limbs supporting it. As I cut limbs off, it would settle a bit and put more and more weight and pressure on those remaining.

I came to a six-inch-diameter limb located at the five o'clock position on the stem, not quite directly on the bottom, but a bit to my side, and I did a miniscule cut to the topside of the limb. I knew there was pressure pushing upward against the limb and that my chainsaw would bind if I cut too much. What I did was not much more than tap it with my saw. This would hopefully allow the branch to break free when I cut on the other side.

That's what I did next. I shifted my feet, got a good stance, and came in with my saw, expecting the limb to release down toward the ground. But it was loaded with wicked tension and a twist that I couldn't see—didn't fathom—and it exploded out from the underside of the tree! With more force than a swung baseball bat, it pounded into my left knee, bending it back in the opposite direction a knee bends, and knocked me to the ground. Sweet, merciful Christ!

I was saved by a four-inch-diameter beech tree that caught the limb and prevented it from folding my knee completely backwards. I think my chainsaw chaps might have helped cushion the blow a little too. No skin was broken so there wasn't any blood to deal with. The pain was excruciating. I couldn't stand up. Didn't even try. It hurt so freakin' bad I started to feel nauseous and light-headed. I just laid still for a while and fought through it. Eventually I pulled out the cell phone I kept fastened to my belt, turned it on and checked for a signal. One bar. I'd left Levi at home, but I doubt he could've gone and told somebody "Timmy fell in a well." Where the hell's Lassie when you need her? I was on my own.

I laid there on my back, staring up at the sky, trying to calm myself down. I ran stuff through my head. "I'm not hurt bad. It's just a little bruise on my knee. ... Take nice steady breaths. ... I'll be fine ... Try to move your leg a little. Wow! Stars came out there for a second. Okay, just rest a bit more ... Sure wish I could get to my water jug on the forwarder. I'm drier than a popcorn fart ... Is that a hawk or a buzzard circling up there? Godfrey, I hope it ain't a buzzard ... Maybe I should call the wife. Nothing she can do. I'll be fine ... Cripes, I'm sweating like a hairy ox. Keep breathing steady. Don't hyper-ventilate ... Should I look at my knee? Hell no! I'll work out of it. Just need to take a little break ... I'll call Karen and just chew the fat for a bit."

I dialed her work number and she picked up her phone.

"Hi Honey! How're you doing?" I asked, trying to sound chipper.

"Good," she said. "Not too busy."

"I was just taking a break and thought I'd give you a jingle. You got a few minutes to spare?"

"Sure. What's up?"

"Not much. Well to be honest, not me. I'm lying here trying not to pass out, so if you could just stay on the line for a bit, it'd be great. I'll be fine. I just had a limb hit my knee and it hurts like the dickens."

"Are you sure you're okay? Where are you? You need help?"

"I'm on the job near Sugarbush. I'll be fine. Just hearing your voice is helping. The pain's getting less. I was bored lying here by myself. I'll work out of it."

"What happened?"

"Oh, I cut off a limb and it went where I wasn't expecting and my left knee took a pounding. I'll be fine."

"You're not bleeding, or anything are you?"

"No. I'm good. I'm feeling better already. I'll call you around noon and let you know how I'm doing."

"You're going to keep working?"

"Yeah. But don't worry. I'm almost done the job. I only have a dozen or so trees left. I'll call you at noon. I love you."

"You be sure to call. And be careful! I love you too."

Being married to a logger isn't without its hazards, but she's a Stark, straight from pioneer stock. It was her kin, General John Stark, who said what became the New Hampshire state motto, "Live free or die!" He didn't leave a whole lot of wiggle room there. She's one of nine kids and I'm fairly certain I got the pick of the litter.

I was finally able to stand up, though still a bit light-headed, and limped over to the dozer where I sat down on the track. I couldn't put much weight on my left leg, and bending the knee hurt like the ol' bloody hairy. But I have a high threshold for pain and a trucker coming to move the dozer on Saturday. I finished out the day. Slow and easy like. Did a little one-legged logging. Went in the next day too and cut the last few trees.

Of course, by the end of the day, my knee had swollen up to the size of a casaba melon and turned all sorts of keen colors from heel to hip. Using that leg to work the clutch on the dozer and tractor brought tears to my eyes. When I got home, my left foot had puffed-up so much I had trouble getting my boot off. I met Jerry early Saturday morning and I escorted my equipment to Trapp Family Lodge and was home by noon. Early Sunday morning, when traffic is the lightest, I took off the tire chains and drove the tractor and forwarder wagon to Stowe. I began the new job Monday morning.

I was still gimping around by the end of the week and, on Karen's insistence, decided to have my knee checked out. I couldn't get in to see an M.D., but I got an appointment with a physician's assistant. She came in the examination room and took a look at my leg.

"Oh my god! What did you do?!"

"I was limbing out a tree and I took a limb on my knee cap a week or so ago. Sort of inverted the joint a might." I explained.

"You did this a week ago? Are you on crutches?" She asked as she scanned around the room for them. "Can you walk?" She seemed concerned.

"Hell, I've been working all week. Been working since it happened. No rest for the wicked." And I gave her a wicked grin.

She then went on to tell me that I had a hyper extension of my knee joint and how I should've been lying still, keeping it iced and elevated. Then she scolded me about the dangers of blood clots that can occur with a severe hematoma such as I had, and that mine was absolutely the worst she'd ever seen. Well that made me feel special, having the best of the worst. Special enough to know I'd worked my way out of it once again.

Chapter 24
At the End of The Haul

The work at Trapp Family Lodge took me through the rest of the summer and deep into the fall. They own thousands of acres. The first section I worked on was near their condominiums. I had to work around a few mountain bike and cross-country ski trails, but nothing that slowed down my production. I would see people during the day, driving by on the road below the landing or on the bike trails nearby in the woods. I had the reassuring feeling that there were others in the area. Civilization was close by and probably within shouting distance.

However, the second area I cut on was on the other side of Tarnation. Haul Road was properly named because it is just that: a freakin' haul. It's a dog path of a road and I was two miles up it—and I mean up. The road went out with a steady climb and an occasional steep grade. After twenty minutes of snaking along in my pickup, I took a turn to the left and went another ten minutes to a landing that had one hell of a view. I pitied the poor bastard driving the truck to get the firewood out and was thankful it wasn't going to be me.

The isolation I felt working in such a distant, out-of-the-way, hard-to-find location kept gnawing at me. If I needed help, I wouldn't get it soon, if at all. As the pile of firewood on the landing increased each day, so did my anxiety, though I wouldn't admit it to anybody. I became more aware of my surroundings. More judicious of my every action. The impression the remoteness put on my psyche felt like a shadow cast over me. It was a heaviness that weighed on me every day as I watched the colors of autumn descend from the high ridges to the valley floor. Fall is the best time to be alive in the woods, and I wanted to stay that way.

Art was in the hospital, so I gave him a call late one afternoon. He'd been in there for a while and this time would be his last. He'd now fought through a dozen operations since we'd bulled and jammed together for eighty cents a tree. He told me on the phone that the doctors had just left his room. Said they told him there wasn't anything else they could do for him. Told him they were sending him home to die.

Hell, I didn't know what to say to him on the phone. What do you say to a man who's been more than a brother to you for most of your life? Stood up for you when you got hitched, as you did for him? Pulled you out of a smoking, mangled car wreck? A man who risked his neck to save mine from certain death beneath a falling beech so many years ago? That steaming hot summer day on the mountain revealed what was really at stake. It opened my eyes to the fact that working in the woods went deeper than a mere job. It taught me that logging, and life, can be a hard school, where the lessons are often given only once.

I've often tried to persuade myself that I did save Art in the woods and just never knew it. I want to believe that some simple thing I did while we were cutting and bunching, sweating and swearing, maybe, possibly, somehow, had broken a vital link in a chain of events—events that were lining up to strike him down. But now death was coming for him, sure as hell, and I couldn't grab him out of the way.

I went to visit him when he got home. We sat and talked while he lay on his death bed. We spoke of many things. There was nothing we left unsaid. We both knew we'd meet again sometime. Knew the grip we'd had on each other. It'll never let go. It reaches beyond this life we shared. Unseen, unwavering.

* * *

A simple awareness occurs in the early days of winter. It usually happens the first few weeks of December, when the weather becomes cold enough to start freezing-in my roads. When it happened, I'd be conscious of Ol' Man Winter daring me to make it through another season. I'd feel it in the first few wisps of snow blown in around my collar. A frozen form of a gauntlet would shake down on me as I scared off a fresh dusting from the limbs hugging the road as I was driving in for the first hitch. I'd see it through the frigid air of a lipstick sunset, painted on the horizon barely past four o'clock. It's a feeling that comes and goes, like a diver taking a deep breath before a long plunge.

Winter came, and with it all the challenges that working in the snowy, frozen landscape had to offer. Though there is boundless beauty to be found in the winter woods, the contrast between what's beauty and what's brutal can be quite severe. On a sub-zero afternoon, I saw a coyote standing a mere twenty yards off my road as I brought out the last load of the day. His face was frosted white; the ripple of his gaunt ribs showed through his thick fur; his eyes, a dull, hungry stare. Deer were feeding heavily in my tops during the day, staying within fifty yards as I worked. Was it just for food, or to gain my protection? There would be hair and blood on the snow in the morning.

The clothing and equipment I put on to work the winter woods weighed near thirty pounds. Each step lifted weight that, by the end of a day, could be measured in tons. Cold, stiff muscles and joints let me know the spring chicken had flown the coop. When March finally came, the feeling that the finish line was close, with spring waiting just beyond, served to nurture my spirit, though many times, deep, nasty March snowstorms blanketed the woods I worked. They came as a final assault from winter, hoping to smother my optimism with a heavy, cold, blanket of white. But I've learned that when you get to the end of the rope, just tie yourself a knot and hold on. Spring will win out.

Twenty years had gone by since I first worked the Vergennes Waterworks with Charlie, and I was back on its sloping hillsides. It was now called the Watershed Center and preserved from development. Its acres were under the management of Vermont Family Forests and David Brynn had me cutting mature hardwood that was ready to harvest. Consisting of mostly red oak and a bit of white ash and maple, it was beautiful timber, and I was grateful to be reaping the fruits of my labor of years long past.

It was the middle of August and I'd just celebrated my birthday. It had been forty years since I picked up a saw and heard the first notes of the beckoning call of the forest. How many thousands of trees had fallen by my hands since then? How many times had danger and death brushed by me, drifting past like the snowflakes of winter, each unique and icy cold?

I was working my way up a ravine with my bulldozer, bunching trees a few hundred feet to my forwarder down below. I had the bulldozer parked in the bottom of the ravine and was cutting marked trees off the banks on either side. I'd cut down a two-foot-diameter rock maple, felling it up the bank of the ravine. I limbed out and topped off the tree and walked back alongside it down the hillside. I paused at the butt of the maple because I noticed a three-inch-diameter hole in the center of what otherwise would've been a nice log. I stood and looked at it for a few moments, making a mental note to cut the log back a couple feet once I got it bunched, to make it a better log.

I turned to continue walking toward the dozer thirty feet away to grab a choker off the rack above the winch. A huge dead stub on the opposite bank came smashing down on the back of the dozer with a sickening thud, smack-dab onto the rack of choker chains. If I hadn't paused for those few, brief moments to look at the maple, I would've been standing there. It would've killed me deader than hell. But a small hole in a maple tree caught my logger's eye in passing, and I'm rewarded with my life.

The chilling reality is there are events that occur in the forest around me that are out of my control, out of my awareness—a truth that's been shrewdly pounded into me for decades. Like dew on the grass beneath a mother's feet, and the hollow emptiness of a girdled beech, they hide in plain sight.

When I finished the work at the Watershed Center, I sold my equipment and left my life as a logger behind. Now I work next door at the golf course, cutting grass instead of trees. And I'd much rather have grass on me than a tree.

Oh, there's still dew on the grass. I just mow right through it.

About Bill Torrey

Bill's family moved to Vermont in 1767. He spent his childhood roaming the fields and forests of his family's farmstead, which led him to a forty-year career of working in the woods. His first book, The Ta Ta Weenie Club was published in 2016. The book contains twenty-one priceless narratives of his upbringing during the '60's and drew vast praise. Bill is also an accomplished oral storyteller. He's won four NPR Moth StorySlams and has performed on the Moth MainStage as well as winning three *Extempo Vt. Storytelling Competitions* and the *VPR Listener's Appreciation Party StorySlam* and the *North Country Public Radio Black Fly StorySlam* and was thus awarded the coveted *Golden Fly Swatter*. He's performed at many venues across Vermont including the *Flynn Theater, The Vermont Folk Life Center, Middlebury College*, the *Vermont State House* and for many private organizations. Bill has written for *Northern Woodlands* magazine, the *Burlington Free Press Writers Group*, and *Outdoors* magazine. Find out more about the author and where he is performing at www.billtorreyvt.com

www.ingramcontent.com/pod-product-compliance
Lightning Source LLC
Chambersburg PA
CBHW071321110526
44591CB00010B/970